ABOUT THE AUTHORS

Dave Hizer is a Detroit-based human resource consultant who dedicates time to working with organizations and individuals on a variety of issues dealing with productivity, planning, and managerial effectiveness.

With over 15 years experience creating and directing managerial and organizational development programs, this enterprising executive reads more resumes in a week than most people skim newspaper headlines in a month. He has authored numerous articles on career planning, self-marketing techniques, and related topics, including "The ABC's of Cover Letters," which appeared in the *Wall Street Journal's* publication, *National Business Employment Weekly.*

The father of two energetic sons, Dave somehow finds the time to conduct national workshops and seminars on motivation, managerial leadership, and career/life planning.

Art Rosenberg is a New York/New Jersey based consultant specializing in user-friendly documentation, corporate communications, and training. His publications include *Chess for Children and the Young at Heart* (Atheneum), a pair of studies on energy management systems (McGraw-Hill), and several journal articles, including "Making the Switch to a High-Tech Job" (*National Business Employment Weekly*).

Writer, inventor, lecturer, translator, and oenophile, this author is a former textbook acquisitions editor (Dun-Donnelly), marketing manager (McGraw-Hill), and international publisher (Harcourt Brace Jovanovich, and the United Nations in Geneva, Switzerland) who is partial to live opera, slow jazz, tournament chess, candlelight cuisine, good grammar, Monday Night Football, long science fiction novels, and short sentences (in no particular order).

THE
RESUME
HANDBOOK

How to Write Outstanding Resumes & Cover Letters for Every Situation

SECOND EDITION – COMPLETELY REVISED

Arthur D. Rosenberg & David V. Hizer

BOB ADAMS, INC.
PUBLISHERS
Holbrook, Massachusetts

DEDICATION

The authors gratefully acknowledge the support and inspiration of Dave's wife Sara, the contributions of Hildegard Hizer, Dr. H, who brought us together, and the editorial staff of Bob Adams, Inc.

Published by
Bob Adams, Inc.
260 Center Street
Holbrook, MA 02343

ISBN: 1-55850-933-X

Manufactured in the United States of America.

10 9 8 7 6 5 4 3

TABLE OF CONTENTS

Preface

The purpose of a resume is *to obtain an interview.*

Your resume is your official representative, a verbal portrait calculated *to arouse an important person's interest in meeting you.*

Your resume is not an autobiographical profile; it's a marketing piece on you. It isn't intended to make people like you or admire you.

Think of your resume as a special tool with one specific purpose: *winning an interview.*

That's right, you've got to go out and *win* your interview, and only the inexperienced and the naive think otherwise. Your resume is a tool designed to get your foot in the doors of companies where you'd like to work. And if you fail to win the interview, you certainly won't get the job.

But there are other resumes out there in competition with your own. So yours must be at least as good as all the others if you're to stand an even chance. Of course, if your resume is *better* it may give you the advantage.

To write an interview-winning resume, you need to know what to say, and how to say it. For this, you need *The Resume Handbook.*

Just as the purpose of your resume is to obtain the interview, the purpose of *The Resume Handbook* is to illustrate successful resume techniques.

The Resume Handbook tells you what kind of information to include in your resume, and what to leave out. Then it provides you with the tools and techniques to present your chosen facts in a convincing and engaging manner.

The Resume Handbook will help you *win the interview.*

The rest is up to you!

INTRODUCTION

After scrutinizing more than 15,000 resumes over a somewhat lesser period of years in professional recruiting work, a single, recurring impression looms large and dominant within our minds: *the overwhelming majority of resumes are overwhelmingly dull!*

Ah, but a veritable work of "art vitae" does happen by on rare occasion, one illuminated with a spark of true, creative thought, and which is pleasing to the eye. Now, if this isn't of itself enough to make our lives exciting, it may at least be interesting to read, and maybe — just perhaps — it will inspire sufficient curiosity to invite the author in for a closer look, which is of course the purpose of a resume.

The purpose of this book is to increase the minuscule percentage of superior resumes, in case we are obliged to read another 15,000 of them prior to retirement.

We've taken great pains to avoid the fat and wordy formats to which most books of this kind are prone. Instead, we've tried to heed our own advice on writing resumes by making our book interesting and to the point. *The Resume Handbook* presents the essential ingredients that go into successful resumes, with lucid explanations and the clearest of examples.

You can read through it in less time than it takes to write a resume, then use it as a reference source when you are ready to begin writing your very own.

Included herein is a chapter on "The 30 Best Resumes We've Ever Seen." You will quickly learn what makes them so effective, and how to apply their winning techniques to your own purposes. The following chapter, "The 5 Worst Resumes We've Ever Seen," illustrates some of the pitfalls to be avoided at all costs, and may prove equally instructive.

The Resume Handbook focuses on three major objectives:

● *Organization:* How to structure and give visual impact to your resume so it immediately captures the reader's attention.

● *The Basic Principles:* What to include and what to leave out of your resume, to avoid wasting the reader's time and running the risk of turning him or her off.

● *Accomplishments:* How to write action-oriented accomplishments by using action verbs, enabling you to represent yourself as a highly-motivated achiever.

We have also included sections on cover letters and personal sales (*broadcast*) letters; they are too important to ignore and are are an essential part of any job-hunting campaign. But our emphasis remains on writing resumes that will enable you to present yourself in the most appealing and engaging manner possible, to help you win the interviews you want.

Art Rosenberg
& Dave Hizer

Chapter One:
Looking for a New Job

Nearly everyone looks for a job at some time in his or her life. The average American worker does so (according to the U.S. Bureau of Labor Statistics) every 3.6 years; according to the National Bureau of Economic Research, Al and Olivia Average work for 10 different employers during their respective lifetimes. In addition, four out of five job-hunters seek to change careers at least once.

Over 40 million of our countrymen are currently involved in some sort of career change or transition. Approximately a third of those now looking for a job are currently employed. Whether this is due to the economy, or the suggestion that a large portion of the working force is under-utilized, the fact remains that competition in the job market is fierce.

Chin up, for all is not entirely bleak. The average firm, for instance, hires nearly as many new workers in a given year as its total number of employees. A construction company with 100 workers may have to hire as many as 200 per year, due to enormous turnover. Service firms with as few as 25 fulltime employees often need to hire 100 or more each year in order to maintain a stable staff.

So if you're looking for a job, you are in excellent company. Naturally you need a system if you are to compete successfully, a technique that will give you an advantage. This is where *The Resume Handbook* can help. For whatever job search methods you may use, you'd better have a darned good resume to penetrate the screening process used by most employers.

WHAT IS A RESUME?

The only valid function of your resume is to get you invited for an interview. It is an advertisement of your skills, experience, and knowledge, presented in their most favorable light.

Your resume precedes you in your job search like an emissary of goodwill. Until you meet the interviewer (if you ever do), the resume is *all* they know of you. Approximately one interview is granted for every 245 resumes received. Obviously, a mediocre resume will rarely win an interview; a poor one hasn't got a chance!

Research tells us that a piece of advertising matter has about a second-and-a-half in which to attract the reader's interest. Someone sitting with a stack of 245 resumes (and probably a whole lot more) is simply not going to accord them equal time. So why not see to it that yours receives the lion's share of the interviewer's attention?

Read on . . . we'll show you how.

WHY WRITE A RESUME IF I'M NOT LOOKING FOR A JOB?

Three reasons:

First, the majority of desirable positions are offered to individuals who are satisfied in their work and who are not necessarily seeking a new job. You never know when opportunity will knock, when the "job of a lifetime" may dangle within your grasp. Thus, it always pays to have an updated copy of your resume at hand for unexpected opportunities.

The second reason is that it can be a valuable experience to observe one's own professional career on paper. Your resume can put your past experience, growth, and goals into perspective, and help chart the path of your future career.

Finally, having a resume can help protect you from the unexpected — losing your job in an economic turndown, for example. A well-prepared resume can take some of the anxiety out of the job search, especially for the experienced professional who suddenly finds him- or herself competing for jobs with young professionals who may be better versed in the latest sophisticated job-hunting techniques.

RESUME ORGANIZATION

There are three commonly-used resume formats:

☐ *Chronological* resumes are safe for people with unbroken records of employment. It's a straightforward, easy-to-follow format (see resume examples 1, 4a, 6, 9, 12, 14, 17, 21, 24, 25, and 27 in "The 30 Best Resumes We've Ever Seen") which includes the dates of current and past employment.

☐ *Functional* (thematic) resumes, unlike chronological ones, focus rather on accomplishments (see examples 2, 3, 4b, 7, 13, 20, 22, 23, and 29). This format is advisable for those with employment gaps due to unemployment, or other activities they might prefer not to reveal (such as jobs from which they were fired or left after a short time, unsuccessful self-employment, prison terms, and a host of other reasons). It is also a better way to emphasize certain aspects of one's career. If, for example, you spent 11 years teaching engineering and only two years as an industrial engineer, a chronological resume would draw attention to your teaching background. But if you happened to be looking for an engineering position within a corporation, the functional format would allow you to play up your industrial experience and de-emphasize the academic side.

Another rationale for choosing the functional approach is if you haven't much to list by way of experience. This tends to be the case with recent graduates, individuals lately discharged from the armed services, and housewives seeking new (or planning to resume) careers after prolonged periods at home.

☐ *Combined* chronological/functional resumes can, when appropriate, offer the best of two worlds (see examples 5, 8, 10, 11, 15, 16, 18, 19, 26, 28, 30).

Each of these resume styles will be demonstrated in intimate detail later in this book. But first:

RESUME PREPARATION

Composing even a brief autobiographical outline requires serious preparation and contemplation. So find a quiet spot (office, den, or dining room table) where you feel comfortable and can be alone and undisturbed. Set aside a period of 4-5 hours, and if possible, unplug the phone.

Collect all the materials you will need, including:

- Pens, pencils, or both — whatever you like using best

- A lined pad (at least 8½ × 11″)

- A good dictionary and a thesaurus

- Records of your past employment, education, and related materials

- Copies of former job applications and correspondence, if available

● Descriptions of some jobs for which you plan to apply

● A copy of *The Resume Handbook*

Now that you're suitably equipped, you can begin to formulate your own *resume strategy.* Be careful to observe the basic principles of resume-writing, which follow next.

Chapter Two:
The Basic Principles of Resume Writing

Writing a successful resume is an art form, with certain basic principles that must always be kept in mind. The following suggestions have been formulated through long years of exposure to all sorts of resumes. Major deviations from these "rules" are at your own creative — and professional — risk.

☐ *Brief is better!* See if you can fit it all on a single page (especially recent graduates and those early in their careers), but don't exceed two pages. Remember, few executives enjoy the task of reading piles of resumes, let alone the thick, voluminous monsters that get mailed out every day.

☐ *Format:* Your name (in bold type or in capital letters), address, and both home and work telephone numbers belong on top. Next come your objectives and summary of qualifications, accomplishments, employment history, education, and related activities and affiliations. Select the resume from the "30 Best Resumes We've Ever Seen" that most closely meets your needs and suits your style, and use it as a model; or combine elements from several of these resume samples.

Education may precede employment history in certain cases, especially if a recent graduate or technical degree is more closely related to the desired position than your employment history. Recent graduates, with little or no work experience, have little choice.

☐ *Optional categories:* These may include career objectives, summary of qualifications, and such personal details as date of birth, marital status, military record, and health. Let's take a separate look at each of these:

● *Career Objectives:* This can be an excellent topic to include if you happen to possess a clear idea of what they are. But general or vague objectives are best omitted. Remember, your objectives can be honed specifically to the job for which you are applying in your cover letter, which we'll address a little later.

Your career objectives must be worded with precision if they are to be included in your resume. They should be clearly stated and consistent with your accomplishments and demonstrated skills, as documented on your resume. Bear in mind the difference between career and job objectives. A career objective is just that . . . a long-range plan that may or may not relate directly to the job for which you are applying. A job objective, on the other hand, is oriented quite specifically to the opening you wish to fill. We recommend using the term "objective" by itself, which would be appropriate for most situations.

● *Summary of Qualifications:* A detailed resume that includes a wealth of professional experience can employ this effectively. The summary may be inserted in addition to, or instead of, a statement of objectives; or the two can be combined ("qualifications and objectives"). At its best, a summary will entice the reader to read further; at its worst, it has the opposite effect. A summary is most helpful if the applicant has had an extremely diversified background, including (for instance) teaching and industry (see "The 30 Best"), or if the resume extends beyond a single page.

- *Personal Data:* If your personal details are "Mom-and-apple pie" and straight as the proverbial arrow, they may lend an air of respectability to your image. However, any non-essential information that you offer is more likely to work against you. Let's face it, prejudices do exist (for example) toward single women, unmarried men over a certain age, and older job-seekers — and why should *anyone* advertise that they're divorced? Your date of birth may only serve to persuade potential employers that you are too young or too old for a given job before they've even met you. Your military record may be worth mentioning if it includes some sort of relevant job training or experience (technical, organizational; see Abel Baker's resume in "The 30 Best"). And finally, who on earth would admit in writing to poor physical (or mental) health? Omit *any* reference to health.

□ Also leave out:

- Reasons for having left a job — they won't enhance your image, and you may create a negative impression.

- Former (or desired) salary — you need to know as much as possible about the job in order to avoid asking for too little or too much. Don't risk putting yourself out of the running before you've even begun.

- Hobbies and memberships in social, fraternal, or religious organizations — potential employers don't need this information, and you never know what may turn them off.

- Reasons for *not* having served in the military.

- Any potentially negative information about you (unless unavoidable), such as prison terms, lost lawsuits, and handicaps that may affect your job performance.

- The label "Resume" or "Vitae" — if the briefest glance does not clearly identify your resume as such, the label will not help.

- The banal "References available on request"; this is taken for granted.

☐ *Visual impact:* Vary type style; use bold type or italics to emphasize key words and subject headings (as discussed in chapter six). If possible, select an off-white paper to help your resume stand out in a stack. Do not send out photocopies; spend a few dollars to have your resume professionally printed or word-processed . . . the difference is well worth the cost. Make sure the resume is *letter-perfect.* Errors, typos, stains, abbreviations (*etc., e.g., i.e.*), technical jargon, and hip or buzz words are strictly taboo. Get your final draft critiqued and proofread by someone reliable.

☐ *Insure integrity:* Poorly written resumes typically lack internal integrity; yours should be consistent. Your job or career objective (if you use one) will be supported by the accomplishments you list. If you are interested in a senior position with an advertising firm, then you should emphasize your accomplishments in management, business development, and in creative programs you've developed. The bottom lime here is that your resume provides separate — but interrelated — facts.

☐ *Employment history:* When writing a chronological resume, strike a balance between job content and accomplishments; the latter should be emphasized (as we'll explain in the next chapter). List your current position first, working back chronologically. De-emphasize the jobs you held further back in time. Avoid verifiable exaggerations that may someday constitute grounds for dismissal. Be sure to use action verbs and phrases to "polish up" the facts to your advantage (see chapter three).

Here's an example of a balanced job history:

```
1979 to Present        Flinthall Electronics, Dover, Ohio.
                       Manager of product testing.  Supervise
                       testing group consisting of 7 research
                       engineers.  Group's mission was to create
                       methods to test performance, safety and
                       durability characteristics of projected
                       products.  While heading up this group:

                       * Initiated testing methods that
                         reduced annual budget of group
                         by 29%.

                       * Received award of excellence for
                         innovations in testing by American
                         Society of Research Engineers-1980.

                       * Increased group efficiency as
                         measured by time and quantity
                         parameters by 35%.

                       * Developed 3 patented testing pro-
                         cedures during last 4 years.
```

☐ *Organizations of which you are a member:* You may safely list the ones that show achievement or professional standing, such as the National Association of Certified Public Accountants, or the Tool & Diemaker's Guild. You can also indicate your leadership abilities as an officer or official in a strictly non-controversial association, like the PTA or Junior Achievement. But stay away from listing political, religious, and potentially controversial groups, because they simply don't belong on resumes.

☐ *Awards:* Be sure to list awards that relate to the kind of job you're seeking, like Pulitzer Prizes, Oscars, or honorary doctorates. Leave out, however, references to having won the league bowling, chess, or karate championship. While these achievements may bolster your ego, they make unwise assumptions about the interviewer. In addition, they have nothing to do with the task at hand — winning an interview.

With these basic resume strategy guidelines in mind, it's time now to focus on the specifics of making *your* resume stand out from the other 244.

Chapter Three:
Stating Your Accomplishments

The *manner* in which you state your accomplishments is no less important than the grim details themselves. Active, energetic phrases attract more of the reader's attention than do dull or passive words. *Created*, for example, sounds more interesting than *began*; *promoted*, *instituted*, and *produced* are much more attention-getting than *worked on*, *became*, or *finished*.

In fact, the very first word you use to describe an accomplishment can make the difference between an impressive resume, and one that's just ho-hum. It may make the difference between its being read or "filed." So before presenting the mechanics of stating your accomplishments in their best possible light, let's pause to digest "Hizer's 57" — a list of action verbs that show you are an *action person*, the kind employers notice.

HIZER'S 57

ACTION VERBS

achieved	directed	organized
administered	eliminated	planned
advanced	established	prepared
advised	evaluated	produced
analyzed	expanded	promoted
authored	focused	provided
automated	headed up	published
coached	identified	reduced
conceptualized	implemented	researched
conducted	improved	restructured
contained	increased	reversed
contracted	initiated	saved
controlled	innovated	scheduled
coordinated	instituted	solved
created	introduced	streamlined
cut	led	supervised
decreased	maintained	taught
designed	managed	trained
developed	negotiated	trimmed

"Hizer's 57" does not pretend to be a complete list of action verbs. These words can, however, be applied to virtually any field or industry, actively demonstrating why your skills would be an asset to any employer. They also help to circumvent the danger of using buzz words, tech-talk, and the like.

Now that you're armed with the right action *verbs*, it's time to turn them into action *phrases* that best demonstrate your accomplishments.

ACTION PHRASES

Dull resumes tend to contain a lot of statements and descriptions that appear to have been copied directly from corporate personnel files. This, of course, is poor resume strategy. A better tactic is to employ phrases stressing your accomplishments in such a way as to attract — and hold — the reader's attention.

An interview-winning resume contains a balance of job content and accomplishments. It also has attention-getting style. You may refer to this as flair, technique, or pizzazz . . . in *The Resume Handbook*, we call it *impact*.

To illustrate the point, here are some contrasting examples of statements often found in resumes. Those on the left are dull; in addition, they tell only half the story: what was done. The action phrases on the right, on the other hand, present a larger context in which to evaluate accomplishments more fully. And they are, indeed, more interesting to read, due in large measure to their effective use of action verbs.

Dull	With Impact
1. Raised level of sales above previous year.	1. Reversed negative sales trend; sales up 41% over prior year.
2. Started new employee programs that lowered turnover.	2. Created and implemented two new employee relations programs (flextime and job posting) resulting in a 33% reduction in turnover.
3. Handled bookings for elderly pop group.	3. Managed bookings, travel, and accommodations for sexagenarian sextet.
4. Housewife of household with six people for past 7 years.	4. Managed and organized six-member household with annual budget of $65,000.

5. Marketed new travel plan to corporations, increasing sales to $19 million.

5. Initiated new market concept of packaging travel to corporations for incentive programs, resulting in sales of $19 million (more than double expectations).

6. Worked for losing gubernatorial candidate for six months.

6. Organized and coordinated political campaign for leading gubernatorial candidate.

7. Opened new sales offices in two cities which broke quotas ahead of schedule.

7. Researched feasibility, then established two new sales offices; both operated above sales quotas within 2 years (6 months ahead of schedule).

8. Hired and trained six new lion tamers during 1987-1989. Only one serious casualty.

8. Recruited, trained, and motivated six new lion tamers during 1987-1989; five continue to excel.

9. Lowered operating costs in my division by $135,000.

9. Initiated cost reducing plan in my division, resulting in 27% ($135,000) cost reduction with no negative effect on production capability.

10. Put on training sessions for supervisors in corporation.

10. Conducted leadership training for 48 supervisory and management level staff members.

11. Increased sales and profitability despite lower budget.

11. Expanded market penetration sales by 14%, and profitability during a period of budgetary cutbacks.

12. Contributed to making group much more efficient.

12. Increased group efficiency as measured by time and quantity parameters by 35%.

13. Wrote ornithology procedures manual for museum.

13. Conceptualized and authored 88-page ornithology procedures manual for museum zoological research department.

In many of the preceding examples, you'll notice a relationship between the action verb used in the phrases with impact, and a more complete and detailed description of accomplishments. This is because action verbs invite further questions — even from you as you are reflecting on your achievements and writing your resume.

Focus on accomplishments that had a noticeable or measurable effect on some part of the establishment where you worked, such as:

- Sales increases, exceeding quotas, expectations, achievements vs. goals, winning recognition for the firm;

- Organization/reorganization/innovation regarding staff, procedures, programs;

- Development of new/innovative professional, management, or marketing strategies and products;

- Projects for which you provided or contributed to leadership;

- Positive results deriving from your actions/proposals.

A careful blend of action verbs and specific accomplishments will get the interviewer's attention. It may motivate him or her to call you in for a serious interview.

Take a look at the following examples and begin thinking of your own accomplishments:

- *Successfully managed*, for past eleven years, a 5-member household with an annual budget of $49,200, while completing Associate of Business degree at Clinton Valley Community College.

- *Researched, wrote and published* information booklet for graduating college seniors: "Don't Pass Go, Don't Collect Up To $200,000 Now."

- *Conceptualized and founded* Meadow Lane Day Care Center, which now cares for 29 children daily.

- *Controlled* expenses on "Parents March for M.S."; treasurer for Imperial and Essex Counties.

- *Organized* food cooperative that purchased $119,000 in consumables during 1989.

- *Created* children's tee-shirt design, then implemented marketing program resulting in gross sales in excess of $70,000.

- *Maintained* 3.9 grade average in business courses at Ohio State University. Completed eleven courses to date.

- *Elected* to represent Nevada State University at the International Congress on Energy Alternatives in Prague, Czechoslovakia.

- *Chosen* over 37 other trainees by senior management as member of four-person management trainee group organized to rewrite the training program we had just taken.

- *Created* neighborhood theatre ensemble which, over the last 9 years, has developed into the nationally renowned "Westgate Orchards Theatre Ensemble."

- *Written up* in Oregon's Eye O-U (Alumni newspaper) as one of ten most promising freshmen in 1982.

- *Initiated* and headed up 90 member "Students for Intellectual Expansion" — University of Missouri's answer to President Carter's challenge to create alternative energy.

- *Conducted* sensitive quality control study for Southeast Michigan Water Authority — written up in Michigan Congressional Record, June, 1987, "Standing Ovation for H_2O."

- *Formed* local Junior Chamber of Commerce, which has grown from 19 to 291 members.

- *Elected* to Board of Directors of the $36 million asset Tri-County Employees Credit Union.

- *Originated* and published "Salescall," an informational newsletter distributed to 144 sales representatives throughout the U.S. "Salescall" covers sales techniques, product knowledge, legislative updates, notes of competition, and technical changes.

- *Headed up* procedures group that eliminated 19 obsolete reports and modified, or combined, 14 others (out of a total of 49) without reducing operational effectiveness.

- *Designed* assembly pivot arm that increased overall line speed by 9%, resulting in an increase in daily production of 39 units (15% increase).

- *Produced* video tape program entitled "Here to Help," outlining Marcot's product servicing capabilities to current and prospective clients.

- *Instituted* self-developed safety program within my production wing of 179 employees, resulting in lost work day savings of 39% over previous 3 years.

The preceding accomplishment statements are action-oriented because they start with action verbs ("Hizer's 57"). All statements are achievement-oriented in that they demonstrate the writer's capability of organizing, completing, leading, and doing. Note that this is accomplished by:

Using quantitative measures to emphasize to what extent the writer completed that achievement. Example: Scored in the 95th percentile on seven out of the eight part state licensing exam for electricians.

Using position to indicate the relative importance of the achievement. Example: Awarded second place out of 60 entrants in the National Collegiate Debate Association "Debate 87" in St. Louis.

Using action verbs to indicate selection over others. Example: Selected fifth for the pre-supervisory awareness program at Big Sky Electric out of 195 candidates.

Using action verbs to indicate leadership in creating, initiating or heading an activity or group. Example: Organized and was first chairperson of Moravia Valley Glass and Can Reclamation Center, which collected 119 tons of recyclable glass and aluminum during 1988. Example: Organized and led 36 member church bazaar group that successfully raised $28,760 over a two year period.

DESCRIBING YOUR EDUCATION

If your employment experience is limited, your educational background may be more relevant to the job you're seeking. In this case, your education will be the initial accomplishment you list. (See examples in the next chapter.) Regardless of whether it is your key accomplishment or subordinate to your job history, there are methods of presenting your educational background concisely and impressively.

For an individual with extensive employment experience, it is usually sufficient to list the bare details:

1980: B.S., Biology, Howard University, Washington, D.C.

or

Cornell University, Ithaca, N.Y.: M.B.A., Business Administration

You may, of course, list any academic honors earned:

1982: San Diego State University, San Diego, California: M.A., History *(cum laude)*.

or

University of New Hampshire, 1984: B.A. in Fine Arts; graduated *summa cum laude*.

If your employment experience is limited, it is a good idea to elaborate on educational achievements before employment:

1989 — Bachelor of Arts Degree in Business Administration, University of Florida. Achieved 3.6 grade average (4.0 scale); specialized in management information systems. Senior project consisted of a 223-page report on the compatibility of selected information retrieval systems. Excerpts were published in July 1988 edition of *M.I.S.*

Boston University, School of Public Communication, 1987. Maintained 3.5/4.0 GPA; emphasized newspaper journalism sequence. While in school, served as editor of *The Daily Free Press* (1985-86); awarded John Scali Achievement Prize for best student investigative news story.

If you have extensive relevant work experience in an academic setting (as do researchers, law students, journalism students and others), be sure to carefully describe that work with action phrases. Limited employment experience also necessitates creativity in describing other educational achievements. A lecture heard at college, work or elsewhere may be described as:

December 1982: Attended seminar on "Business Computer Languages" at RETI School of Electronics, Rapid City, SD.

Summer 1988: Participated in weeklong seminar on publishing procedures and marketing techniques, University of New Mexico.

List any relevant certificates you've earned:

Received "Fortran Programming Proficiency" certificate from ABC Business Institute, Phoenix, AZ: February, 1989.

Awarded certificate of proficiency in "Business Communication Machinery" from Control Info Institute, 1988.

If you lack a college degree, emphasize any classes attended or years completed. This can be worded so as to suggest you're in the process of completing a degree:

UNIVERSITY OF MIAMI (Evening Division): B.S., Mathematics; in progress.

or

Currently working on B.S. Degree in Public Administration, University of Delaware.

People with a lot of professional experience commonly list the seminars, lectures, or certificate programs they have attended, and so should you. This will help to mitigate any negative impressions your lack of a degree might create.

Those who haven't earned college degrees are advised to list their high school diplomas. For example:

1968: Diploma (with honors), Davis High School, Mt. Vernon, N.Y.

or

Graduated 1983 (college preparatory courses); Edgewater High School, Orlando, FL.

□ □ □

Following these guidelines on stating your accomplishments, your resume should fairly *sing* to an employer: *call me in for an interview; I can help your company.* Remember, your resume is all they know of you until you walk through that door. The only way an employer can identify you as an action-oriented individual is from your resume, and action verbs will help you to accomplish this objective.

Having mastered the art of using action verbs, your remaining task is a mechanical one: plugging these action phrases into the following general format.

When stating your accomplishments, be sure to include:

- Name and location of the organization (city/state only; street address is unnecessary)

- Specific job title

- Job description

- Skills applied

- Skills acquired (if applicable)

- Significant accomplishments

- Dates of employment (unless using functional format)

In listing former jobs, it is recommended that you go back no more than 10-12 years, unless you've spent all that time with the same company; in that case, briefly list an earlier job or two.

Gaps in employment dates of more than a month or two should, if possible, be "hidden" (or satisfactorily explained: sabbatical to complete degree, illness, military service, etc.) by extending dates of earlier and later employment, or even better, by employing a functional format.

Once you've stated your accomplishments using action verbs and phrases that embellish your performance, you've completed the most difficult part of writing an effective resume.

Ready to begin? Before you do, we suggest you take a look at chapters four and five, to see how others have created their masterpieces . . . and disasters.

Chapter Four:
The 30 Best Resumes We've Ever Seen

The following resumes, appropriately edited and modified (in order to protect the authors), are among the best we've yet discovered. Selected from more than 15,000 resumes inspected over a period of years, these examples pull together the various techniques we've been discussing. Each one deals with a specific, real-life situation. There are examples here for just about every situation, and there are elements from each that you may want to consider incorporating into yours.

These 30 resumes are organized into the three categories we looked at earlier:

- Chronological: This type of resume is fairly straight-forward; eleven examples are included (see resume examples 1, 4a, 6, 9, 12, 14, 17, 21, 24, 25, and 27).

- Functional: This category allows for a great deal of variation (see resume examples 2, 3, 4b, 7, 13, 20, 22, 23, and 29).

- Combined: Here we apply the best of both techniques (see resume examples 5, 8, 10, 11, 15, 16, 18, 19, 26, 28, and 30).

Good work speaks for itself, so we present these exemplary resumes intact. The concepts that make these resumes stand out are noted in the margins.

Each resume is labeled by format (chronological, functional, combined) and general background of the user. Nevertheless, they are intended to serve as good examples of just about any career-oriented resume, and the lessons from each can be applied to your own uses.

Resume Example #1: An imaginative and creative "blue-collar professional" looking for a better job.

PIERRE CUISINE

MASTER CHEF

14 Fourchette Boulevard
New Orleans, Louisiana

Telephone (mornings)
(504) 555-0544

The proper blend of training and diversified experience is my recipe for culinary excellence!

From the everyday to the extraordinaire, when your clientèle have tasted my international entrées they will demand "encore."

CREATIVE OBJECTIVE FOR A CREATIVE BUSINESS.

EXPERIENCE
1984–
Present

Arnaud's Restaurant   Head Chef
New Orleans, Louisiana

EVIDENCE OF MANAGEMENT ABILITIES AND EXPERIENCE.

Manage entire kitchen staff of 22 that produces the finest luncheons and dinners in the South.
* Create extraordinary seafood, meat, and chicken dishes, specializing in delicate sauces.
* Supervise 3 assistant chefs and wine steward.
* Oversee training of 4 apprentices.
* Responsible for purchases of all foods.

1979–
1984

Le Chateau   Chef
Charlesbourg, Quebec

One of 2 chefs directly under head chef.
* Prepared special sauces and such delicate specialties as pheasant-under-glass.
* Served flambees and other spectacular dishes in dining room.

1975–
1979

Chez Paul Beaucoup   Apprentice Chef
Paris, France

THE TYPE OF TRAINING THAT STANDS OUT.

* Prepared hors d'oeuvres, entrées, and desserts under the direction of one of the world's foremost chefs.
* Assisted in the purchase of foods and kitchen supplies.

EDUCATION
1975

Diploma, Ecole d'Haute Cuisine, Lyons, France. Generally recognized as the leading cooking school in Europe.

MAKES AN IMPORTANT POINT THAT MIGHT OTHERWISE BE OVERLOOKED.

SPECIAL TALENTS

* Capable of serving as knowledgeable wine steward.
* Fluent French and English; spoken Italian and Spanish.
* Aware of kosher dietary laws.

PERSONAL

Dual Nationality: French and Canadian.
Willing to relocate anywhere in the world.

CLEVER, WITTY, APPEALING.

CHRONOLOGICAL

Resume Example #2: Unemployed, but with solid office skills and a record of steady employment.

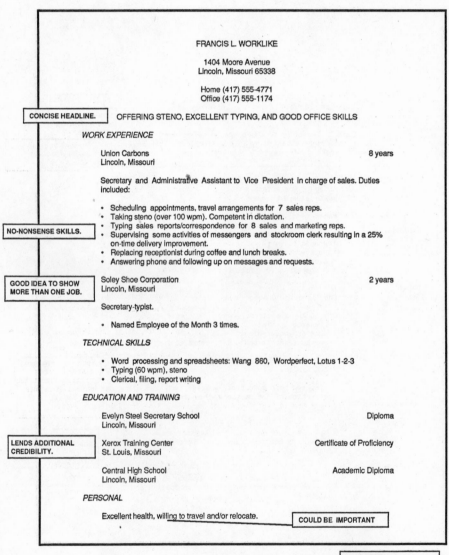

FRANCIS L. WORKLIKE

1404 Moore Avenue
Lincoln, Missouri 65338

Home (417) 555-4771
Office (417) 555-1174

CONCISE HEADLINE. OFFERING STENO, EXCELLENT TYPING, AND GOOD OFFICE SKILLS

WORK EXPERIENCE

Union Carbons   8 years
Lincoln, Missouri

Secretary and Administrative Assistant to Vice President in charge of sales. Duties included:

NO-NONSENSE SKILLS.

- Scheduling appointments, travel arrangements for 7 sales reps.
- Taking steno (over 100 wpm). Competent in dictation.
- Typing sales reports/correspondence for 8 sales and marketing reps.
- Supervising some activities of messengers and stockroom clerk resulting in a 25% on-time delivery improvement.
- Replacing receptionist during coffee and lunch breaks.
- Answering phone and following up on messages and requests.

GOOD IDEA TO SHOW MORE THAN ONE JOB.

Soley Shoe Corporation   2 years
Lincoln, Missouri

Secretary-typist.

- Named Employee of the Month 3 times.

TECHNICAL SKILLS

- Word processing and spreadsheets: Wang 860, Wordperfect, Lotus 1-2-3
- Typing (60 wpm), steno
- Clerical, filing, report writing

EDUCATION AND TRAINING

Evelyn Steel Secretary School   Diploma
Lincoln, Missouri

LENDS ADDITIONAL CREDIBILITY.

Xerox Training Center   Certificate of Proficiency
St. Louis, Missouri

Central High School   Academic Diploma
Lincoln, Missouri

PERSONAL

Excellent health, willing to travel and/or relocate.   **COULD BE IMPORTANT**

NO FRILLS, BUSINESSLIKE APPROACH TO GETTING A JOB.

FUNCTIONAL

50

Resume Example #3: High-tech!

Mike Rochip

3380 Disk Drive
Silicon Valley, GA 30314

Residence (404) 555-2628
Business (404) 555-9284

OBJECTIVE: *[SOLID OBJECTIVE.]*	To provide systems programming services in a major DP complex; to upgrade the skills of systems programming staff through specialized training.
SUMMARY: *[STRONG CREDENTIALS.]*	Over twenty years of data processing experience encompassing all aspects of operating systems: Installation, Service, Diagnostics, Design, Development, Testing, Build/Integration, Project Leadership, Prototyping, Research, Education, and Consulting. *[IMPRESSIVE TECHNICAL KNOWLEDGE AND SKILLS.]*
HARDWARE:	IBM 303x, 308x, 434I, 438I, S/370, S/360, IBM PC.
SOFTWARE:	MVS/XA, MVS/SP, VM/370, TSO, CMS, ISPF, SMP/E, JES2, JES3, VSAM, BDAM, IMS, RACF, ICF, IDCAMS, DF/EF, RMF, DFP, IPCS, NJE, IPO/SIPO.CBIPO, UCC7, VS/1, OMEGAMON, SAM-E, VTAM, TCAM
LANGUAGES:	S/370 BAL, PL/1, APL. BASIC, PASCAL, REXX, FORTRAN

[ACTION WORDS TELL WHAT HE'S DONE.]

PROFESSIONAL ACHIEVEMENTS

Design:	• Wrote design specifications for major components of three operating systems.
Development:	• Led technical team for development of major MVS component.
Prototyping:	• Designed, coordinated, and implemented 20K LOC prototype for major component of MVS.
Negotiation:	• Coordinated design efforts and strategic directions of four IBM divisions for a major VM component.
Testing:	• Wrote, coordinated, and tracked component test plan for MVS Supervisor (OS/VS2 Release 2).
Integration:	• Key technical planner in development of build plan for OS/VS2 Release (MVS).
Installation/	• Converted three data centers from MVS/SP to MVS/XA.
Maintenance:	• Installed and serviced the following major systems and system components:

[ACHIEVEMENTS CLEARLY CATEGORIZED.]

MVS/XA	MVS/SP	VM/370	IMS/VS
TSO/E	VTAM	JES 2	JES3
RACF	DFP	DF/EF	TCAM
ISPF	NJE	RMF	3270/Session Mgr.
TSO	UCC7	DMS/OS	
APL/SV			

[MEANINGFUL DETAILS TO TECHNICAL EMPLOYERS.]

and numerous additional program products.

Planning:	• Specified and justified hardware/software systems in support of growth and changing demands of education department for IBM's Data Systems Division.

-continued-

FUNCTIONAL

Resume Example #3 continued

Mike Rochlp   Page 2

Tuning:	• Supervised performance measurement and tuning of MVS installation containing interactive (IMS, TSO, APL.SV, and IIS) and batch. Accomplished both in a native and VM production guest environment.
	• Led division task force to reduce path length in paging-related components of MVS (OS/VS2 Release 2); impacted five system components, resulted in path-length reduction in excess of 25%.
	• Headed IBM corporate task force to solve MVS V2CR problem.
Instruction:	• Created and taught courses in Languages, DB/DC, operating systems, teleprocessing, and system diagnostics.
	• Designed/developed productivity enhancing software tools:
	• IMS to TSO interface (interactive DL/I).
	• Full-screen editor for IBM 2250 (1981).
	• Interactive system of programs to plan, model, and schedule.
	• Designed and taught seminars on effective use of visual aids (videotaped and used as standard training aid for IBM instructors and managers).
	• Developed and taught electronics specialty upgrade courses for SAC headquarters electronics technicians.
Technical Publications:	• "MVS-VM/370 Cohabitation — Making the Marriage Work" • "Dynamic Generation and Control of Large Data Bases for Interactive Systems Testing" • "Large System Effects in MVS" • "Cache Cross-Interrogate Effects in an N-Way MVS System"
Software Patents:	• "Dynamic Quickcell Function" — status = file

> **A SPECIAL CATEGORY OF EXPERIENCE.**

> **THE ICING ON THE CAKE.**

EDUCATION: Clemson University
MA - Systems Analysis
1975

Georgia Tech
BA - Mathematics
1971

PROFESSIONAL
ORGANIZATIONS: ASM, DPMA, IEEE

Resume Example #4a: A former academic, who has made the jump into the world of business.

V. KING BRACE

42 Community Circle   Home: (904) 555-4090
Orlando, Florida 32801   Office: (904) 555-9409

EMPLOYMENT
EXPERIENCE

5/86 - Present   Barfield & Ivanovich, Inc.   Senior Editor of
                   Orlando, Florida   Social Studies and History

                   Acquisition and publication of professional/reference textbooks.

| COST SAVINGS. |
                   • Canceled 20 outdated and unwanted contracts without expense or litigation, saving an
                     estimated $500,000.
                   • Revamped existing list of social studies texts, more than doubling revenue over a 2-year
                     period.
                   • Established and published a profitable selection of history books, leading to the creation of
                     new Assistant Editor position.

8/82 - 4/86   Hazard House Publishing   Social Sciences Editor
                   New York, New York

                                                          | SPECIFIC
                                                            ACHIEVEMENTS. |
                   Acquisition and publication of college textbooks.

                   • Redefined short- and medium-range publishing priorities in fields of psychology and
                     sociology.
                   • Increased profitability of list by 44% during a period of budget reductions.
| MANAGERIAL | • Improved communications between editorial and sales staff, resulting in largest single year
  ACHIEVEMENT.   sales increase in 11 years.

9/76 - 6/82   New York University   Assistant Professor of Psychology
                   New York, New York

                   • Conducted graduate and undergraduate classes in behavioral and clinical psychology. | ACADEMIC. |
                   • Initiated liaisons between department and college publishing houses, resulting in 50-60
                     graduate students serving as management reviewers.

RELATED   Consultant to Hazard House Publishing Company while teaching at
PROFESSIONAL   New York University.
ACTIVITIES
                   Advisor to New York State Behavioral Research Center.

-continued-

CHRONOLOGICAL

Resume Example #4a continued

PUBLICATIONS   1987: "Behavior in an Industrial Society" (with Dr. I.H. Feuerbach) - Barfield & Ivanovich.

RELEVANT TO   1985: "The Inhuman Time Bomb" (edited readings) - Irving Press.
ACADEMIA
AND PUBLISHING.   1978-1988: Twenty-two articles and monographs in professional journals (including "The
                              Behaviorist") and popular publications (including "Psychology Tomorrow").

EDUCATION   1976: Ph. D., Clinical Psychology, University of California at Los Angeles.

                    1973: M.A., Industrial Psychology, Kent State University, Kent, Ohio.

                    1971: B.A., Psychology, Youngstown State University, Youngstown, Ohio.

FOREIGN   German
LANGUAGES   COULD DELETE.

54

Resume Example #4b: Here is the same person as in #4a, but with his background presented functionally.

V. KING BRACE

42 Community Circle
Orlando, Florida 32801

Home (904) 555-4090
Office (904) 555—9409

OBJECTIVE

TO THE POINT.

The editorial directorship of a major social sciences and humanities publishing department in higher education.

SUMMARY OF QUALIFICATIONS

Over six years of highly successful editorial acquisitions, including extensive experience in: product development, planning, budgeting, marketing, management, staff supervision and training, with Barfield and Ivanovich (Orlando) and Hazard House (New York).

EMPHASIZES PUBLISHING BACKGROUND.

PROFESSIONAL ACHIEVEMENTS

Product Development

COMPLETE STATEMENT.

• Published highly profitable selection of academic textbooks, increasing revenue by more than 100% (over a 2-year period) and increasing profitability by 44% (during a period of budget cutbacks).

Planning and Budgeting
• Established editorial priorities for one and five year plans, including budget requirements and projected revenues.
• Saved an estimated $500,000 by canceling outdated and unwanted contracts without expense or litigation

ACCOMPLISHMENTS ARE PLACED IN A MEANINGFUL CONTEXT.

Marketing
• Produced accurate and meaningful data for marketing and sales staff, contributing to exceptionally high sales increase.

Management Supervision and Training
• Coordinated work-flow of copy and production editors, publishing schedules, and daily interaction with more than 25 authors.
• Supervised two junior acquisitions editors, both of whom were subsequently promoted.
• Implemented visible and successful on-the-job training program for editorial assistants.

RELATED PROFESSIONAL ACTIVITIES

Assistant Professor of Psychology, New York University.

Consultant to Hazard House (while teaching).

DOWNPLAYS ACADEMIC BACKGROUND.

Advisor to New York State Behavioral Research Center.

-continued-

FUNCTIONAL

Resume Example #4b continued

PUBLICATIONS

    1987: "Behavior in an Industrial Society" (with Dr. I.H. Feuerbach) - Barfield & Ivanovich.

    1985: "The Inhuman Time Bomb" (edited readings) - Irving Press.

    1978-1988: Twenty-two articles and monographs in professional journals (including "The Behaviorist") and popular publications (including "Psychology Tomorrow").

EDUCATION

    1976: Ph. D., Clinical Psychology, University of California at Los Angeles.

    1973: M.A., Industrial Psychology, Kent State University, Kent, Ohio.

    1971: B.A., Psychology, Youngstown State University, Youngstown, Ohio.

FOREIGN
LANGUAGES
    German

Resume Example #5: Leaving the military; seeking a career in business.

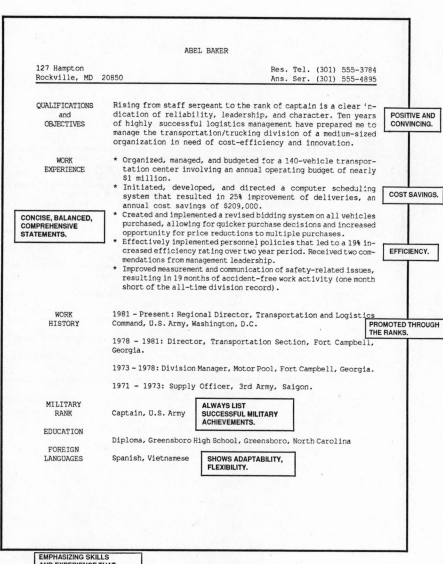

ABEL BAKER

127 Hampton
Rockville, MD 20850

Res. Tel. (301) 555-3784
Ans. Ser. (301) 555-4895

QUALIFICATIONS and OBJECTIVES	Rising from staff sergeant to the rank of captain is a clear indication of reliability, leadership, and character. Ten years of highly successful logistics management have prepared me to manage the transportation/trucking division of a medium-sized organization in need of cost-efficiency and innovation.	**POSITIVE AND CONVINCING.**

WORK EXPERIENCE

* Organized, managed, and budgeted for a 140-vehicle transportation center involving an annual operating budget of nearly $1 million.
* Initiated, developed, and directed a computer scheduling system that resulted in 25% improvement of deliveries, an annual cost savings of $209,000.　**COST SAVINGS.**
* Created and implemented a revised bidding system on all vehicles purchased, allowing for quicker purchase decisions and increased opportunity for price reductions to multiple purchases.
* Effectively implemented personnel policies that led to a 19% increased efficiency rating over two year period. Received two commendations from management leadership.　**EFFICIENCY.**
* Improved measurement and communication of safety-related issues, resulting in 19 months of accident-free work activity (one month short of the all-time division record).

CONCISE, BALANCED, COMPREHENSIVE STATEMENTS.

WORK HISTORY

1981 - Present: Regional Director, Transportation and Logistics Command, U.S. Army, Washington, D.C.　**PROMOTED THROUGH THE RANKS.**

1978 - 1981: Director, Transportation Section, Fort Campbell, Georgia.

1973 - 1978: Division Manager, Motor Pool, Fort Campbell, Georgia.

1971 - 1973: Supply Officer, 3rd Army, Saigon.

MILITARY RANK

Captain, U.S. Army　**ALWAYS LIST SUCCESSFUL MILITARY ACHIEVEMENTS.**

EDUCATION

Diploma, Greensboro High School, Greensboro, North Carolina

FOREIGN LANGUAGES

Spanish, Vietnamese　**SHOWS ADAPTABILITY, FLEXIBILITY.**

EMPHASIZING SKILLS AND EXPERIENCE THAT ARE OF INTEREST TO POTENTIAL EMPLOYERS; DE-EMPHASIZING THOSE THAT ARE LESS SO.

COMBINED

57

Resume Example #6: A hospital care specialist demonstrates his versatility and broad range of skills.

SHERMAN N. JECTION

1 Maywood Road   Residence: (804) 555-0001
Roanoake, VA 24014   Business: (804) 555-1000

EXPERIENCE: *MEDICAL CARE ASSOCIATES*, Asheville, NC
October 1988   GENERAL MANAGER
to Present

Directly responsible for all operations of a Medicare certified home health agency with annual revenue of $4,200,000. Major services include: Home health care, private duty care, and supplemental staffing. 900 full and part-time employees; 5 branch offices.

DEMONSTRATES ORIENTATION AND VALUE OF MANAGEMENT ACTION.

• *Reorganized* internal operations, resulting in monthly savings of $10,000
• *Implemented* marketing programs and internal controls that resulted in 20% increase in sales.
• *Managed* successful transition from franchise operation to corporate branch.
• *Directed* implementation of computerized client and employee information system.

March 1978 to   *WALTER A. CUMMINS HOSPITAL SYSTEM*, Mobile, AL
October 1988   DIRECTOR OF MANAGEMENT SERVICES
                        BEAUMONT SHARED SERVICES, INC.
                        (October 1987 to October 1988)

Responsible for several major components of $30,000,000 per year for profit subsidiary of hospital. Responsibilities included: contract management, management consulting, strategic planning, business development, home health care.

HAS AN EYE FOR EARNINGS.

• *Planned and implemented* establishment of durable medical equipment subsidiary; generated over $400,000 in revenue. $40,000 in profit during first year.
• *Initiated* first comprehensive strategic planning process for Cummins Shared Services.
• *Expanded* contract management to include four hospitals and various consulting projects; generated revenue in excess of $200,000 per year.
• *Designed* comprehensive wage and benefit program for Shared Services employees; reduced personnel expenses by 15%, but maintained current staffing levels.
• *Invited* to speak as guest lecturer for Alabama Hospital Association on hospitals and home health care.

ASSISTANT DIRECTOR
(September 1986 to October 1987)

Complete administrative responsibility for patient support departments of 950-bed teaching hospital. Responsible for 520 employees and annual budget of $6,600,000.

VERSATILE AND ADVENTURESOME.

• *Planned* and helped initiate conversion of former school into comprehensive outpatient health center.
• *Organized* and conducted major consulting projects in Nigeria and Saudi Arabia.
• *Initiated* the planning process required to streamline functions of patient service departments.

-continued-

LAYS IT ALL OUT CLEARLY AND WITH DETAIL.

CHRONOLOGICAL

Resume Example #6 continued

ARKANSAS COMMUNITY HOSPITAL, Little Rock, AR
ADMINISTRATOR
(September 1984 to August 1986)

Full responsibility for 25-bed acute care hospital with annual budget of $2,500,000.
• *Developed* and implemented comprehensive business plan and budget system.
• *Successfully* recruited two family practitioners to hospital's service area.
• *Successfully* negotiated vendor contracts that reduced expenses by 10%.

NORTH VIRGINIA HOSPITAL SYSTEM, Arlington, VA
ADMINISTRATIVE ASSOCIATE
(February 1982 to August 1984).
Responsible for management functions of Clinical Pathology Department, which employed 250.
Areas of responsibility included: fiscal management, laboratory and employee representation to
administration, operational policies and procedures.

PERSONNEL ASSISTANT
(November 1980 to January 1982)
Responsible for provision of personnel services to all areas of hospital. Developed department's
data processing systems. Administered wage and salary and grievance programs.

FINANCIAL ANALYST
(March 1978 to October 1980)
Assisted in preparation of revenue, expense and capital budgets. Prepared and analyzed
monthly variance reports and financial statements. Managed hospital's investment portfolio.

February 1975   *WOODWORTH DEPARTMENT STORE*, Washington, DC
to March 1978   FINANCIAL ANALYST
                  Two year active duty military obligation fulfilled during this period.

MILITARY   *U.S. ARMY*
SERVICE: (March 1976 to March 1978)
                  Stationed at Pentagon. Honorable discharge.

EDUCATION: M.B.A. — Howard University, 1982. Hospital Administration.
                  M.A. — Jackson State, 1980. Guidance and Counseling.
                  B.S. — Morgan State, 1973, Economics and Business Administration.

AFFILIATIONS: American College of Hospital Administrators (member).

Resume Example #7: An ex-offender who has changed his ways makes even the worst of his experiences work for him.

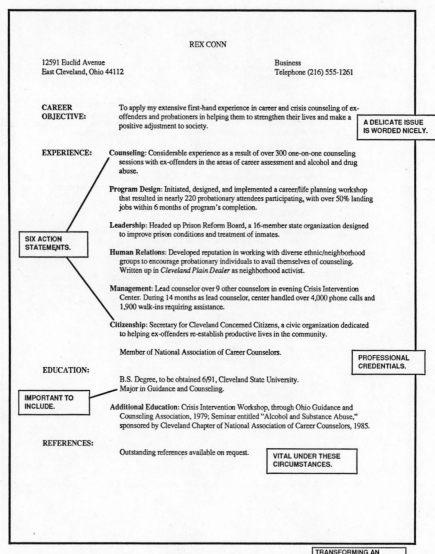

REX CONN

12591 Euclid Avenue
East Cleveland, Ohio 44112

Business
Telephone (216) 555-1261

CAREER OBJECTIVE: To apply my extensive first-hand experience in career and crisis counseling of ex-offenders and probationers in helping them to strengthen their lives and make a positive adjustment to society.

> A DELICATE ISSUE IS WORDED NICELY.

EXPERIENCE:

Counseling: Considerable experience as a result of over 300 one-on-one counseling sessions with ex-offenders in the areas of career assessment and alcohol and drug abuse.

Program Design: Initiated, designed, and implemented a career/life planning workshop that resulted in nearly 220 probationary attendees participating, with over 50% landing jobs within 6 months of program's completion.

Leadership: Headed up Prison Reform Board, a 16-member state organization designed to improve prison conditions and treatment of inmates.

> SIX ACTION STATEMENTS.

Human Relations: Developed reputation in working with diverse ethnic/neighborhood groups to encourage probationary individuals to avail themselves of counseling. Written up in *Cleveland Plain Dealer* as neighborhood activist.

Management: Lead counselor over 9 other counselors in evening Crisis Intervention Center. During 14 months as lead counselor, center handled over 4,000 phone calls and 1,900 walk-ins requiring assistance.

Citizenship: Secretary for Cleveland Concerned Citizens, a civic organization dedicated to helping ex-offenders re-establish productive lives in the community.

Member of National Association of Career Counselors.

> PROFESSIONAL CREDENTIALS.

EDUCATION:

B.S. Degree, to be obtained 6/91, Cleveland State University. Major in Guidance and Counseling.

> IMPORTANT TO INCLUDE.

Additional Education: Crisis Intervention Workshop, through Ohio Guidance and Counseling Association, 1979; Seminar entitled "Alcohol and Substance Abuse," sponsored by Cleveland Chapter of National Association of Career Counselors, 1985.

REFERENCES:

Outstanding references available on request.

> VITAL UNDER THESE CIRCUMSTANCES.

> TRANSFORMING AN UNFORTUNATE EXPERIENCE INTO A POSITIVE AND OPTIMISTIC CAREER.

FUNCTIONAL

Resume Example #8: An administrator planning a career change.

ELLEN McSELLWELL

310 El Camino Real
San Diego, California 92103

Res. Tel. (619) 555-0000
Bus. Tel. (619) 555-0001

OBJECTIVE

Hospital and medical sales requiring extensive experience with state-of-the-art medical equipment, outstanding communications skills, and strong motivation.

PARTICULARLY IMPORTANT TO STATE OBJECTIVE WHEN CHANGING CAREERS.

PROFESSIONAL ACCOMPLISHMENTS

• Successfully conducted training seminars for nearly 200 supervisory personnel in interpersonal skills.

CLEVER STATEMENT.

• Developed reputation for simultaneously coordinating numerous involved projects. Written up in Hospital Administrator magazine, 1980.

• Retained by 3 directors. Appointed to current position over 14 other qualified candidates.

COMPETITIVE.

• Achievement-motivated, conscientious, objectives directed. Obtained highest perfo~~rmance rating for~~ 3 years.

SALES-ORIENTED.

• Adept at problem resolution and public relations. Regularly represent hospital at major civic gatherings.

• Experienced in the development of management systems, including the administration of a $4.3 million budget.

• Received U.S. security clearance.

EMPLOYMENT HISTORY

1982 - 1989: Administrative Assistant to the Director, San Diego Memorial Hospital.

1978 - 1982: Administrator to the Chief of Medical Administration, San Diego.

1976 - 1978: Sold LaBelle health and beauty products door-to-door in West Virginia

EDUCATION

B.A., Administrative Management
Marshall University, Huntington, West Virginia

Additional course work at University of San Diego in Group Dynamics, Management, and Psychology.

NICE TOUCH.

ADDITIONAL EDUCATION

Job Enrichment . . . Hospital Supervision . . . Advance Management Conference . . . Kepner-Gregoe Problem Solving . . . AMA Supervisory Skills . . . T.A. for Supervisors.

PERSONAL

Able and willing to relocate and/or travel extensively.

KEY STATEMENT FOR ANYONE WANTING TO BREAK INTO SALES.

UTILIZING SKILLS AND ACCOMPLISHMENTS TO CONSTRUCT A NEW CAREER.

COMBINED

61

Resume Example #9: A research scientist who isn't looking for a job, at present.

GINO A. LOGICO

29 Vauxhall Road   Work: (317) 555-1587
Indianapolis, IN 46250   Home: (317) 555-9229

**EMPLOYMENT
HISTORY**

August 1987   *Wallace Labs*   **RESEARCH SCIENTIST**
to Present   **Indianapolis, IN**

                    Research and coordinate development of enzyme immunoassays for diagnostic products. Responsibilities
                    include developing and implementing protein purification procedures, enzyme-antibody conjugates, and
                    solid phase technology for EIAs. Develop scaleup procedures to be used in manufacturing diagnostic
                    products.

January 1981   *Academic Press*   **PRODUCTION/PROJECT EDITOR**
to August 1987   **New York, NY**

                    Coordinated production (scientific treatises and textbooks) from manuscript to bound book. Participated
                    in planning of marketing strategies.

                    Edited and rewrote technical material.

November 1978   *American Institute of Physics*   **COPY/PRODUCTION EDITOR**
to January 1981   **New York, NY**

                    Controlled production of *Review of Scientific Instruments*, a monthly journal.

                    Rewrote and edited technical manuscripts.

EDUCATION
September 1982   *Indiana Medical Center*   **Ph. D IN PHARMACOLOGY**
to June 1988   *Indiana State University*
                    Bloomington, IN

                    Past five years have included extensive laboratory research and experimentation in the following areas:
                    Drug receptor studies   Drug-induced changes in enzyme activity
                    Regulation of *in vitro* cell proliferation   Protein biochemistry
                    HPLC (attended seminar course)   Enzyme purification

September 1974   *University of Illinois (Downstate)*   **B.S. IN BIOLOGY**
to June 1978   **Urbana, Illinois**

                    Graduated summa cum laude; 3.81 cumulative index.

                    Elected to several honor societies; received Dean's Award for scholastic excellence.

-continued-

> **GOOD, APPEALING ACTION VERBS.**

> **CLEAR AND EASY TO READ.**

> **WORTH MENTIONING.**

CHRONOLOGICAL

Resume Example #9 continued

PUBLICATIONS

IMPORTANT FOR A RESEARCHER.

March 1988: *Biochemical Pharmacology* (Vol. 34, No. 6., pp. 811-819). Title: Effect of streptozotocin on the glutathione S-transfers of mouse liver cytosol.

August 1985: *Journal of Laboratory and Clinical Medicine* (Vol. 100, No. 2, pp. 178-185) Title: Identification of a glucocorticoid receptor in the human leukemia cell line K562.

November 1984: *Blood* (Vol. 58., No. 5, Suppl. 1, p. 120 (a). Abstract; same title as article above.

RELATED ACTIVITIES

Downstate: Instruction of medical students in pharmacology.
U. of IN: Tutored undergraduate students in science and mathematics.

SPECIAL SKILLS

Computer literate.   **NICE ADDITION.**

PERSONAL DATA

Married, two children.

UNNECESSARY, BUT CAN'T HURT.

Resume Example #10: A graphic design professional tracks his progression into management.

MICHAEL ANGELO

3000 South Valley View Boulevard
Las Vegas, NV 89102

(702) 555-9999

WELL STATED OBJECTIVE.

OBJECTIVE   Management position in visual communications where strong operations management, graphic design capacity, and ability to develop staff will contribute to the productivity and profitability of the organization.

PROFESSIONAL SUMMARY   Versatile graphic design professional with 30 years of marketing-oriented experience including production management, two- and three- dimensional graphic problem solving, staff development, logistic sensitivity, in-depth knowledge of reproduction systems and long-standing record in creative resolution of customer needs.

OBJECTIVE SUMMARY BACKED BY DETAILS THAT FOLLOW.

SIGNIFICANT ACCOMPLISHMENTS

BROKEN DOWN INTO CATEGORIES.

Management, Operations

• Restructured production organization of 190 employees with 15 supervisors on three shifts to 170 employees with 11 supervisors on two shifts while accommodating 20% increase in sales and workload.

SPECIFIC MEASURABLE ACCOMPLISHMENTS.

• Streamlined procedures integrating related creative functions under fewer supervisors. Created multi-skilled technicians to avoid overstaffing. Annual profit increased from $65,000 to $750,000 in two years.

• Reversed operating losses in group producing $360,000 in annual sales. Increased group sales to $1,365,000. Workforce reduced from 11 to 8; group is now a profit leader.

• Authored purchasing/receiving/inventory control program to reduce inventory on hand by 50%, to $225,000. Upgraded requisition system from numbered adhesive tags to electronic entry. Revision allowed first accurate P&L reports.

Management, Human Resources

• Instituted revolutionary employee evaluation procedure to include employee in performance analysis, goal setting, and determination of wage adjustment. Ninety-five percent of employees rated themselves more critically (and requested smaller wage increases) than under previous system.

• Eliminated historic animosity between first and second shift personnel through structured team activity and promotion concept of "16-hour work cycle" to replace existing attitudes of two competing shifts.

• Identified critical system failure — order writers not trained in production methods and capabilities. Over 20% of orders impossible to complete as written. Instituted scheduled training program; erroneous orders still declining.

-continued-

COMBINED

MICHAEL ANGELO   Page 2

Creative Problem Solving
• Conceived, developed, and produced photographically generated color sample booklets to resolve client frustrations when specifying photographic color from process ink samples in standard PMS color swatch books.

• Produced 12-foot-high black and white mural from vertical crop of 16mm movie frame; heavily retouched intermediate 20" x 24" print. Copy negative of retouched print produced mural in three sections through fine mezzotint screen. Mural still on display.

• Provided display text in Arabic, German, and Russian using New York-based translation services and foreign-language typesetters. Obtained necessary entry permits and approvals; produced export documents. Arranged pre-paid services.

• Produced full-color mural to be self-supporting in traveling use as backdrop for mall fashion shows. Mural in sections, plus supporting devices, fit into carrying case less than 36" x 36".

Program Design
• Consulted with over 200 varied clients in need of A/V programs of all types, sizes, and budgets. Advised appropriate use of overhead transparencies vs. 35mm, computer, or optical slices; guided style and format selection. Produced roughs or storyboards from scripts or notes.

• Restructured production system and quotation to produce environmental graphics for client hospital when original quote of $400,000 proved beyond budget tolerance. Project completed for $160,000.

• Managed graphic production of major space museum project at Jackson Community College. Schedule allowed six weeks from receipt of text, NASA transparencies, and artifacts to opening. Installation completed prior to opening.

EMPLOYMENT HISTORY

1987-1989	**Wonderfully Creative**	Director of Production
1981-1987	**Graphic Designs, Inc.**	Manager, Design and Display
1970-1981	**Somewhat Creative**	Graphics Manager
	Designs, Ltd.	Director of Show Services
1959-1970	**Detroit Edison Company**	Export Manager
	Graphic Designer	Account Representative

MANAGEMENT DEVELOPMENT PROGRAMS

Statistical Process Control — Oakland U.
The Deming Method — G. Washington U.
Investment in Excellence — Pacific Inst.
Effective Team Facilitation — J. Farr
American Economic System — Oakland U.
Managing Stress — R. Goren
Communicating for Action — T. Stafford
Statistical Though Process — Beta Assoc.

CLEVER WAY TO COVER LACK OF COLLEGE DEGREE.

EDUCATION   Advertising Design — Center for Creative Studies, 1968

Resume Example #11: A middle-aged executive looking for a top-management spot.

Eleven Cordial Avenue
Ridgefield Park, NJ 07660

Home (201) 555-9876
Office (201) 555-0001

PULLING ALL THE ELEMENTS TOGETHER; IMPACT, SKILLS, ACCOUNTABILITY, EXPERIENCE, SUCCESS.

NOAH A. LOTTS

OBJECTIVE: Senior Most Corporate Planner, General Manager, or Chief Marketing Officer.

POWERFUL STATEMENT.

DIVISIONAL VICE PRESIDENT — Profit and loss responsibility for corporation with annual sales volume of $76 million. Corporation acquired by growing conglomerate resulting in restructured sales organization, leading to expanded market reach. Developed new market strategy, added new sales representatives, dropped 2 unprofitable products and added 3 new products. Strategy allowed for 21% sales increase and profit increase of $3.7 million.

MARKETING, PRODUCTION, and GENERAL MANAGEMENT
- *Initiated* and *managed* design and implementation of new product line with eventual sales record of $12.7 million over first two years.
- *Developed* and *implemented* three year plan to upgrade efficiency of extensive line operation including a capital expenditure commitment of $9.3 million.
- *Decreased* $900,000 accounts receivable collections from 87-day average to less than 35 days.
- *Initiated* improving scheduling system resulting in reduction of delivery time by half.

VICE PRESIDENT CORPORATE PLANNING
- *Introduced* "Results Oriented Management" (MBO) approach to $750 million insurance company that led to a bottom line increase of 29% during a down economy.
- *Developed* and *implemented* $310 million acquisition program over 5 year period utilizing stock/tax advantages leading to R.O.I. improvement of 19%.
- *Created* product development group, which delivered 6 new insurance programs over 3 year period leading to sales of $19 million and profit of $31 million.

INNOVATIVE.

CHIEF MARKETING OFFICER
- *Conceived* of and marketed credit card program leading to $131 million in gross revenues over 4 year period.
- *Developed* award-winning advertising program with annual budget of $9 million.
- *Revamped* product line that suffered loss of 15% in market share, resulting in recapture of 27% of market over 3 1/2 year period.
- *Reorganized* 47 member sales organization, allowing for increased field time and reduced travel, and resulting in a decrease in sales expenditures of $1.5 million in 1 year.

EMPLOYMENT HISTORY
1973 - 1989	Quadrangle International, Hoboken, NJ
1969 - 1973	Gotham Insurance, Inc., Wilmington, DE
1961 - 1969	Metal Specialties Corp., Syracuse NY
1951 - 1956	First National Bank, Hartford CT

SOLID.

IT WOULD BE DIFFICULT TO FORMULATE MORE IMPRESSIVE ACCOMPLISHMENTS THAN THESE.

MILITARY SERVICE — 1949 - 1951. U.S. Army, 1st Lieutenant, Communications.

EDUCATION — B.A. — New York University, 1948 — Business Administration.

PROBLEM-SOLVING.

FOREIGN LANGUAGE — Spanish

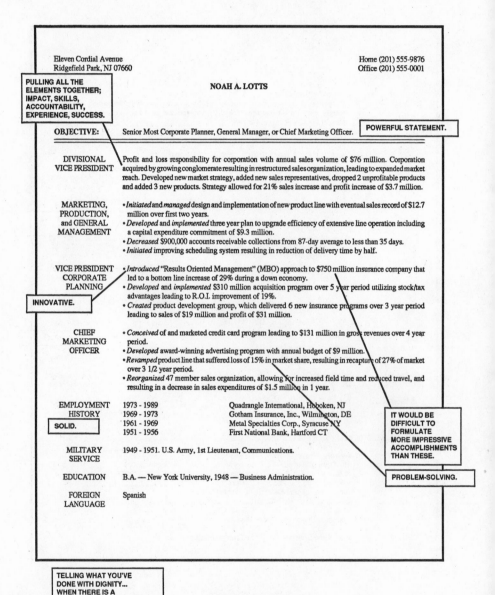

TELLING WHAT YOU'VE DONE WITH DIGNITY... WHEN THERE IS A GOOD DEAL TO TALK ABOUT.

COMBINED

66

Resume Example #12: An engineer with well-chosen accomplishment statements and a marketing flair.

JULIO IGLESIAS GARCIA

1001 Asuncion   Tel.: 807/555-2333
San Juan, PR 00920

EMPLOYMENT   Carib Electro Corporation, San Juan — Service and Quality Control Manager. Responsible for
1985   field and customer service activities along with quality control inspection of equipment to insure
TO   compliance with customer, OSHA, and JIC standards. Additional responsibilities include pur-
PRESENT   chasing and technical service manual writing.

> * Organized 6-person service department to perform SAE certification testing verification of
>   systems, resulting in 60% increase in contract revenues, along with warranty and non-warranty
>   repairs leading to a 45% increase in repeat sales.

ATTENTION:
PROSPECTIVE
EMPLOYERS.

> * Wrote technical operation and maintenance manuals for all systems manufactured.

> * Reduced purchasing costs by 32% by developing and utilizing purchasing program for TRS80
>   computer.

BOTTOM-LINE
ORIENTED.

1981   ABZ Corporation, Xeroradiography Division—Technical Specialist. Responsible for field service
TO   and support of all technical representatives and contractors within designated region.
1985

> * Promoted from technical representative in Ponce branch to specialist within 9 months of
>   employment; became responsible for San Juan territory.

> * Reduced nationwide service call rate by developing and implementing various in-field system
>   retrofits.

> * Relocated to develop new area in Denver-based territory, resulting in area sales increase of 35
>   systems the following year.

GETS RESULTS.

EDUCATION   New York University, November 1980 — Bachelor of Applied Science, Electronic Engineering
                  Technology. Graduated with 3.95/4.0 G.P.A.; primary concentrations in business communica-
DRAWS OUT BUSINESS tion, personnel administration, human resource management, business law, principles of
AND HUMAN BEHAVIOR marketing and behavioral psychology.
CLASSES.

                  RETS Electronic, June 1978 — Associates Degree in Electronic Engineering Technology.
                  Second Class FCC Radio Telephone license.

ACTIVITIES   Participating member of Society of Technical Communication (STC).

SPECIAL   Bilingual (English/Spanish)   ESSENTIAL FOR
SKILLS   THIS LOCATION.

CHRONOLOGICAL

Resume Example #13: A mid-level manager looking to make a substantial jump in responsibility.

ERIC VON HOHAUSER

79 Brampton Street   Res. 701/555-1001
Bismarck, ND 58010   Bus. 701/555-0110

PROFESSIONAL EXPERIENCE: Seventeen years of administrative and sales management in finance and insurance.

HIGHLIGHTS SALES AND PRODUCT MANAGEMENT CAPABILITIES.
As Financial Services Manager for Life Enhancement Insurance Co., responsible on a national basis for new account installations, new business development, and marketing of financial products. Conduct seminar presentations to potential customer groups on a variety of financial topics relating to our product capabilities. Extremely knowledgeable concerning all phases of consumer lending regulations. Headed up project and marketed microcomputer system that has now been installed in over 300 credit unions. Designed and implemented an IRA product that has been sold to over 100 credit unions in first six months.

While at Laurel Schools Credit Union, was Operations Officer directly responsible for internal operations of this $22 million financial institutions with 33 employees. Was Chief Operating Officer; personally administered all lending activities, accounting, staff training, loan delinquencies, and work flow scheduling. Implemented revolving credit loan system. Designed marketing promotions and more efficient services resulting in assets increasing from $10 million to $22 million in two years.

POINTS OUT GENERAL MANAGEMENT EXPERIENCE.

GOOD FINAL PARAGRAPH THAT COVERS A VARIETY OF ADMINISTRATIVE TALENTS.
While at Manufacturers Mortgage, originated and handled underwriting for short-term commercial construction loans; supervised $20 million portfolio. At Monroe Bank and Trust, designed operating procedures for branch office and main office departments. Developed procedures for implementation of Master Charge system, conducted training sessions with over 300 branch personnel. Conducted analysis resulting in purchase and installation of such equipment as high-speed check photographing machines, branch camera equipment, and teller machines.

COMMUNITY ACTIVITIES:

Chairman, Administrative Committee for St. Michael's Parish.

Member, Citizens Advisory Group for Board of Education.

EDUCATION:

B.B.A., 1975, University of Miami, Business Administration.

EACH OF THE 3 PARAGRAPHS ILLUSTRATES A SET OF SKILLS THAT HIGHLIGHTS THIS INDIVIDUAL'S VERSAILITY.

FUNCTIONAL

***Resume Example #14:** A senior-level executive who effectively highlights her successes in the international arena.*

CONSTANCE WORLDLY

1696 South Fourth Street
Philadelphia, PA 19147

Residence: (215)321-2121
Messages: (215)321-3232

OBJECTIVE

Resourceful, results-oriented executive accustomed to profit and loss responsibilities seeks domestic or international marketing position, preferably in high-tech materials manufacturing.

BACKGROUND SUMMARY

Extensive experience principally at executive level in international and domestic marketing, manufacturing and engineering research and development, for $115 million manufacturer of precision specialty metal products. Strengths in development of production facilities and licensees in Europe and the Far East. Distinguished record in new product development and patents. Solid background in managing start-up and on-going production operations.

CAREER HISTORY

Monolithic Industries, Philadelphia, PA   1975 - Present

Vice President, International Operations: 1982 - Present

Direct overseas marketing and licensees in Europe and Asia for manufacturer of bearings and friction materials. Annual revenue from licensees up to $25 million.

* Instructed Japanese licensee on bearing manufacturing processes including powder-making, strip sintering and related operations. Increased license fees by 315% per year.

* Designed and arranged financing for $16 million bearings manufacturing plant in India generating a $5.5 million profit on $14 million in equipment sales.

* Researched market, established process, and designed manufacturing facility for low cost production of cam bushings in mainland China for $37 million world-wide market..

General Manager, Bearings Division: 1984 - 1987

Profit and loss responsibility for all operations, including manufacturing, quality, engineering, finance, personnel and marketing. Annual sales $60 million. Staff of 800 in four facilities.

* Restructured division on a product line basis generating an additional 8% gross margin, reducing inventory $3 million and increasing profits by $2.5 million from a loss position in first year of operation.

-continued-

CHRONOLOGICAL

Resume Example #14 continued

CONSTANCE WORLDLY

CAREER HISTORY: (continued)

* Directed start-up of production at 100,000 square foot manufacturing plant.

* Increased market share to 60% at 3 major automobile companies in a declining market.

Director of Sales and Marketing: 1979 - 1984

Directed marketing program for OEM bearings and transmission parts. Annual sales: $75 million.

| PROGRESSION OF RESPONSIBILITIES. |

* Organized and staffed complete marketing activity. Sales growth compounded at 17% per year ($10 to $40 million) in 9 years; non automotive sales increased 300%.

* Established European licensees resulting in a $9.5 million equipment order in Rumania, licensees in France and Germany, plus new major customer accounts.

Director of Research and Development: 1975 - 1989

Directed materials research, process development and customer engineering activities.

* Developed unique asbestos-free, paper-based friction materials generating $15 million sales (60% gross profit).

* Analyzed process for sintering of copper-lead on steel strip yielding a 300% increase in output and 40% cost reduction for a $11 million annual savings.

Alloys, Incorporated, Jennings, Iowa   1968 - 1975

| MORE THAN TEN YEARS PAST, BUT SHOWS SOLID TECHNICAL BACKGROUND. |

Research Metallurgist: Studied wear and fatigue properties of metals. Developed new materials involving the sintering and casting of non-ferrous metals.

EDUCATION

University of Nebraska - B.S., Physics and Mathematics

Advanced Management Training courses on Manufacturing Strategy at Harvard University Business School and at Iowa State University Graduate School of Sales and Marketing

PATENTS and PUBLICATIONS

| A PROSPECTIVE EMPLOYER WILL WANT TO KNOW THE DETAILS IN AN INTERVIEW. |

Twenty-one patents dealing with materials and processes.

Numerous articles in a variety of technical and marketing publications.

ASSOCIATIONS

Society of Automotive Engineers - American Society for Metals

Resume Example #15: A credit manager highlights his creativity and proven ability to create new business.

ADAM SMITH

19008 Holparken Square
Des Moines, IA 50336

Residence: (515) 555-0001
Business: (515) 555-0002

ADMINISTRATION and MARKETING
CREDIT MANAGEMENT . . . PRODUCT PROMOTION
HOUSING . . . RECREATIONAL PRODUCTS . . . EXPORTING

> AN EFFECTIVE ALTERNATIVE TO THE CAREER OBJECTIVE: CALLS ATTENTION TO SKILLS, CAPABILITIES, AND INDUSTRY EXPERIENCE.

An entrepreneurial manager with strong credit background who has worked closely with company marketing personnel in setting up a solid dealer organization. Experienced in working with federal and state agencies and top management to adapt and promote the company's products.

SIGNIFICANT ACCOMPLISHMENTS

Credit Management
- Implemented "private brands" finance program with vice-president of marketing to make program more understandable and to speed up paperwork process.

- Prevented potential loss of $110,000 by moving quickly and securing debtor's business property to insure debt payment.

- Served on finance committee of Manufactured Housing Institute for several years; coordinated activities with federal agencies (HUD, FHA, and VA) on housing matters.

> THESE SUPPORT "CAREER" HEADING AND PROVIDE INTERNAL INTEGRITY.

- Testified for company at 12 trials involving legal and bankruptcy proceedings against former accounts.

- Knowledgeable in Uniform Commercial Code and all necessary filings required to protect company's security interest in inventory.

Marketing
- Promoted company's product lines through European trade office of State of Michigan by providing literature and quotations to interested foreign firms. Six requests for proposals resulted.

- Initiated concept and promoted "Ways to Be a Successful Dealer" to 400 mobile home dealers at national mobile home show seminar.

- Instrumental in selling $650,000 of repossessed inventory of specially built tractor-trailer equipment at no loss to employer.

- Established land-home sales program for dealers in Southeastern United States with national finance company, resulting in over $500,000 in additional business.

-continued-

COMBINED

71

Resume Example #15 continued

ADAM SMITH   Page 2

Creative Programs
- Generated additional sales and profits by inviting trade specialist from U.S. Department of Commerce to advise top management on promoting products overseas.

- Persuaded Builders Credit to perform additional credit investigation program on new dealer applicants in order to reduce future losses.

- Initiated credit interchange program with 12 other credit managers within industry to identify problem accounts and reduce potential losses.

SUPPORTS HEADING AND SHOWS VERSATILITY.

- Developed (with top management and U.S. Department of Commerce's Jamaican office) moderately priced housing units to meet housing needs of hurricane devastated Jamaica.

EMPLOYMENT HISTORY

1977-1989	Labor Division Home Builders Co.	Credit Manager
1971-1977	Nationswealth National Bank	Assistant Credit Manager
1968-1971	Laissez-Faire, Inc.	Sales and Leasing Representative

EDUCATION

B.S. Finance — University of Scotland, 1968
Completed 10 credits toward M.B.A. at University of Detroit, 1970-71

Resume Example #16: An upbeat, creative presentation of an impressive track record in big-ticket marketing.

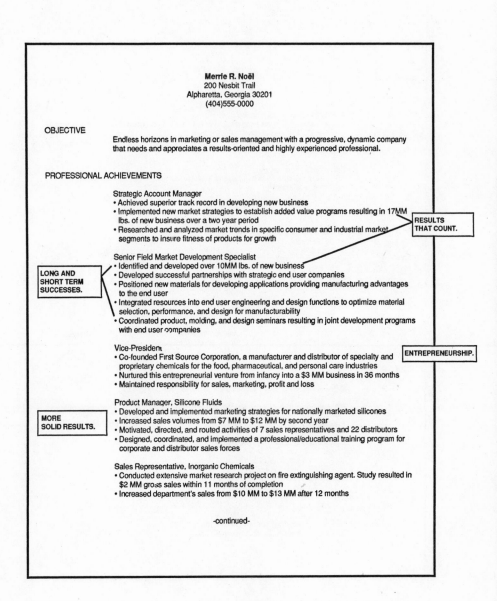

Merrie R. Noël
200 Nesbit Trail
Alpharetta, Georgia 30201
(404)555-0000

OBJECTIVE

Endless horizons in marketing or sales management with a progressive, dynamic company that needs and appreciates a results-oriented and highly experienced professional.

PROFESSIONAL ACHIEVEMENTS

Strategic Account Manager
- Achieved superior track record in developing new business
- Implemented new market strategies to establish added value programs resulting in 17MM lbs. of new business over a two year period
- Researched and analyzed market trends in specific consumer and industrial market segments to insure fitness of products for growth

RESULTS THAT COUNT.

Senior Field Market Development Specialist
- Identified and developed over 10MM lbs. of new business
- Developed successful partnerships with strategic end user companies
- Positioned new materials for developing applications providing manufacturing advantages to the end user
- Integrated resources into end user engineering and design functions to optimize material selection, performance, and design for manufacturability
- Coordinated product, molding, and design seminars resulting in joint development programs with end user companies

LONG AND SHORT TERM SUCCESSES.

Vice-President
- Co-founded First Source Corporation, a manufacturer and distributor of specialty and proprietary chemicals for the food, pharmaceutical, and personal care industries
- Nurtured this entrepreneurial venture from infancy into a $3 MM business in 36 months
- Maintained responsibility for sales, marketing, profit and loss

ENTREPRENEURSHIP.

Product Manager, Silicone Fluids
- Developed and implemented marketing strategies for nationally marketed silicones
- Increased sales volumes from $7 MM to $12 MM by second year
- Motivated, directed, and routed activities of 7 sales representatives and 22 distributors
- Designed, coordinated, and implemented a professional/educational training program for corporate and distributor sales forces

MORE SOLID RESULTS.

Sales Representative, Inorganic Chemicals
- Conducted extensive market research project on fire extinguishing agent. Study resulted in $2 MM gross sales within 11 months of completion
- Increased department's sales from $10 MM to $13 MM after 12 months

-continued-

COMBINED

Resume Example #16 continued

Assistant to Director of Marketing
- Coordinated product evaluations/approvals with major U.S. customers for for eight products sold to U.S. licensees abroad.
- Conducted extensive market research projects to assist in developing product strategies for U.S. market

Buyer, Import Purchasing
- Directly responsible for purchasing $75 MM of products (raw material ingredients and imported resale items)

EMPLOYMENT HISTORY

HF PLASTICS, Pittsfield, Massachusetts: 5/86 to present

9/88 to present	Strategic Account Manager
1/87 to 9/88	Senior Field Market Development Specialist
5/86 to 1/87	Field Market Development Specialist

FIRST SOURCE CORPORATION, Cedar Hills, Illinois: 4/83 to 5/86

4/83 to 5/86	Vice-President

POUNE-ROLANC, INC., Tillamook Junction, New Jersey: 9/75 to 4/83

1/82 to 4/83	Product Manager, Silicone Fluids
1/80 to 1/82	Sales Representative, Inorganic Chemicals
12/78 to 1/80	Assistant to Director of Marketing, Organic Chemicals
10/76 to 12/78	Buyer, Import Purchasing

EDUCATION

B.A. — Education, French: University of Delaware, 1974

Management Seminars: American Management Association: 1989
Industrial Market Research: 1987
Purchasing: 1987

SHOWS WILLINGNESS TO KEEP ON LEARNING.

Communispond: Effective Presentations: 1988

HF Plastics Management Development Institute

Modern Marketing Course: 1988
Product Planning Course: 1989

AWARDS

HF Plastics Marketing Division Award — 1987
HF Plastics Marketing Division Award — 1988

74

Resume Example #17: A high-level executive who gets it all onto a single page.

ROGER M.B. AIMAN

14 McCaul Street
Toronto, Ontario M5T 1W1

home (416) 555-1514
office (416) 555-8285

Professional
Experience

1983-
Present

PUBLISHERS ASSOCIATED SERVICES, INC., Toronto, Ontario
President & Principal — Promote and furnish cost-efficient microcomputer systems to publishing companies. Assist in selection of appropriate hardware and software designed to save time, control costs, increase editorial and marketing productivity

> HE SAYS A LOT WITH A FEW WELL-CHOSEN WORDS.

1980-
1983

THOMAS PUBLICATIONS, Toronto, Ontario
President & CEO — Chief executive in charge of operations for a leading vocational/technical textbook publisher. Exercised P&L authority for all phases of management, including editorial, production, and marketing, with 70 employees reporting.

Executive Vice-President — Reporting to the Chairman of the Board.
Administered daily operations of Mardel Publishers in Albany, NY. Position combined general management authority with supervision of marketing and sales staff. Established computerized sales information systems, resulting in better allocation of sales territories and improvements in capital investment in publishing projects.

> WHEN YOU HAVE ACCOMPLISHED THIS MUCH, DETAILS CAN BE SAFELY SUMMARIZED.

Director, Marketing & Sales — Directed all marketing activities, including advertising, direct mail promotion, product releases, exhibits, and field selling. Developed computer data base of mailing lists, and organized sales communication system for timely reportage by field sales representatives.

O'BRIEN-HULL BOOK COMPANY OF CANADA, Toronto, Ontario
Held key positions in Marketing & Sales Administration with three textbook divisions: Goutt, Collegiate Community, and Vocational/Technical. Achievements include development of first integrated product information system for college and technical/vocational titles; introduced Professional Selling Skills program to college travelers; designed and published Technical Education News quarterly magazine; instrumental in converting catalogs to computer data base for electronic typesetting.

Education

1978 — MBA, University of Toronto Graduate School of Business Administration

1975 — BA, McGill University, Montreal

CHRONOLOGICAL

Resume Example #18: A recent college graduate who makes an excellent representation of her brief but relevant work experience.

BEVERLY BARLEYCORN
147 Deerwood Lane
Cedar Rapids, IA 52404
(309)555-0001

OBJECTIVE
A position in financial administration, financial analysis, financial planning, or funds management that will require my best efforts.

EDUCATION
B.A., Financial Administration, June 1990
Iowa State University
GPA: 3.5/4.0

PROFESSIONAL EMPLOYMENT
Summers 1988 & 1989: Holt Corp., Alpha Insulation Division, Iowa City.

THREE WELL-WRITTEN STATEMENTS DEMONSTRATING A BROAD RANGE OF EXPERIENCES.

- *Financial Analyst:* Analyzed operating, pricing, and purchasing variances weekly. Prepared financial performance reports. Provided financial analysis for special projects. Took part in year-end closing and LIFO cost calculations. Attended budget and forecasting meetings with senior management. Interacted in various controllership duties.

- *Inventory Control:* Planned and conducted verification systems for the Direct Salesforce to report status of inventories accurately. Audited and reconciled inventories of the vans, mini-warehouses, and regional warehouses. Recommended methods to reduce inventory shrinkage.

- *Credit Analyst:* Responsible for USA Direct Sell operations. Approved or rejected sales orders from customers. Reviewed and revised customer credit limits. Wrote 80-page procedure manual for the Credit Department to help establish a consistent credit policy. Negotiated special rates with the collection agencies.

POSITIONS HELD WHILE ATTENDING COLLEGE

1986-1990 (part-time): Iowa State University
Student Assistant: Duties included processing journals, checking out assigned reading and general books, door checking, and shelving books.

1987 (summer): March Companies, Inc., Iowa City
Route Driver: Vacation relief driver; also filled in for terminated salespeople. Responsibilities included selling, delivering, accounting, banking, inventory control, and customer services.

1986 (summer): Karmond Lumber Co., Cedar Rapids
Customer Service: Assisted customers in filling their orders, trained new employees, stocked merchandise, took inventories, and made deliveries to customers' homes.

1985 (summer): Cambridge Condominiums, Cedar Rapids
Maintenance Person: Duties included landscaping and general maintenance.

WELL-PHRASED STATEMENTS THAT MAKE THE MOST OUT OF EACH POSITION.

HONORS AND ACTIVITIES

DEMONSTRATES LEADERSHIP AND ACHIEVEMENT MOTIVATION.

Dean's Honor List — seven terms
Volunteer Income Tax Assistance
Iowa State Finance Club Membership Director
Gamma Phi Nu Fraternity
Intrafraternity Council Representative

A WELL THOUGHT OUT RESUME THAT MAKES MAXIMUM USE OF THIS INDIVIDUAL'S OFFERINGS.

COMBINED

76

Resume Example #19: A highly experienced, versatile, professional manager who puts his best foot forward.

CHRISTOPHER LIBIDOS

42 East 73rd Avenue
Tulsa, OK 74115

Home: 405/555-0000
Office: 405/555-0001

ABILITY TO IDENTIFY, FORMULATE, AND MARKET HIGH PAYOFF PROJECTS:
Developed projects that led to birth of 6,000 terminal communications network, $20 million-a-year wholesale company (the Arbor House Specials seen on TV), installing M.B.O., annual marketing plan in division of 1450, and an accounting system for bookstores.

ABILITY TO START, GROW, AND MANAGE DEPARTMENTS: Started and managed: 5 training departments, research department, personnel department, and district sales office. Played key role starting 70 national account sales departments and 2 research departments.

P&L RESPONSIBILITY: Started division with $66,500 budget; now over $2.8 million.

ABILITY TO WORK AT TOP LEVELS: Setting up board summit meetings to develop corporate objectives. Directly responsible to board for several projects. Staff person in charge of several board committees. Sold and serviced group coverage working with top management and unions of major companies. Three years as Management Consultant.

SCOPE OF TRAINING EXPERIENCE: Managing and doing: Sales training, management and organizational development, plus clerical and technical training. Developing, staffing, and selling 50 workshops with 5,000 enrollees per year, throughout North America, regarding: financial and marketing management. Producer of workbooks, movies, programmed instruction and video programs.

SCOPE OF RESEARCH EXPERIENCE: Managing: Market research, new product development, operations improvement, R&D, and fact base development and maintenance. Create and conduct census of retail flower shops; primary source of data for floral industry.

POSITIONS:

1986 - Present	Director, Education and Research Division, Arbor House. International association; 1200 retail bookstores.
1983 - 1986	Management Consultant for consulting firm of Martell and Coxwell, Inc. Worked with National Association of Healthcare Affiliates, Timon Mufflers, and Oceanic Airlines.
1981 - 1983	Manager, Employee Development Department, Ohio Healthcare Affiliates.
1976 - 1981	Manager of various sales, training, and personnel functions, including the Automobile Club of Ohio.
EDUCATION:	B.A., Economics, Washington State University, Seattle, Washington. Over 1500 classroom hours at: University of Tulsa, University of Chicago, Ohio State University. Re: Management, Mathematics, Organizational Development, Behavioral Science, and Educational Technology.

Annotations:
WELL-PHRASED HEADINGS.

COMBINATION OF EXPERIENCES SHOWS BOTH VERSATILITY AND DEPTH.

EMPHASIS HERE IS ON CONTINUING EDUCATION.

HERE'S ADDITIONAL PROOF THAT A ONE-PAGE RESUME CAN PROVIDE IMPACT.

COMBINED

Resume Example #20: Transforming "housewifery" into job-related skills.

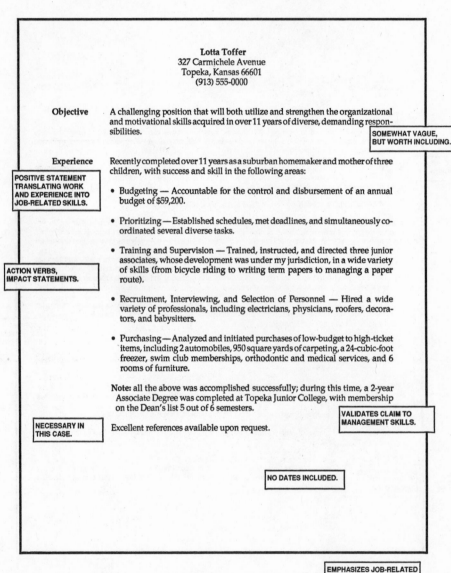

Lotta Toffer
327 Carmichele Avenue
Topeka, Kansas 66601
(913) 555-0000

Objective — A challenging position that will both utilize and strengthen the organizational and motivational skills acquired in over 11 years of diverse, demanding responsibilities.

> **SOMEWHAT VAGUE, BUT WORTH INCLUDING.**

Experience — Recently completed over 11 years as a suburban homemaker and mother of three children, with success and skill in the following areas:

> **POSITIVE STATEMENT TRANSLATING WORK AND EXPERIENCE INTO JOB-RELATED SKILLS.**

- Budgeting — Accountable for the control and disbursement of an annual budget of $59,200.

- Prioritizing — Established schedules, met deadlines, and simultaneously coordinated several diverse tasks.

- Training and Supervision — Trained, instructed, and directed three junior associates, whose development was under my jurisdiction, in a wide variety of skills (from bicycle riding to writing term papers to managing a paper route).

> **ACTION VERBS, IMPACT STATEMENTS.**

- Recruitment, Interviewing, and Selection of Personnel — Hired a wide variety of professionals, including electricians, physicians, roofers, decorators, and babysitters.

- Purchasing — Analyzed and initiated purchases of low-budget to high-ticket items, including 2 automobiles, 950 square yards of carpeting, a 24-cubic-foot freezer, swim club memberships, orthodontic and medical services, and 6 rooms of furniture.

Note: all the above was accomplished successfully; during this time, a 2-year Associate Degree was completed at Topeka Junior College, with membership on the Dean's list 5 out of 6 semesters.

> **VALIDATES CLAIM TO MANAGEMENT SKILLS.**

Excellent references available upon request.

> **NECESSARY IN THIS CASE.**

> **NO DATES INCLUDED.**

> **EMPHASIZES JOB-RELATED SKILLS AND ACHIEVEMENTS.**

FUNCTIONAL

Resume Example #21: A legal specialist provides in-depth details.

LEON R. LAWLESS

40 Orchard Avenue
Ogden, UT 84404
(801) 555-1389

NOTHING FANCY HERE;
STRAIGHTFORWARD
FACTS TELL IT ALL.

EXPERIENCE

1983-present   **WEDMAN, GIBBONS, GOLDMAN & MOORE**
(1981 spin-off from Moran, Sullivan, Forrest & Yee)
Ogden, UT   ASSOCIATE ATTORNEY

TECHNICAL DETAILS
LIKE THESE ARE
REQUIRED FOR
PROFESSIONS SUCH AS
LAW.

Conduct all aspects of patent prosecution, including: patentability evaluations and validity opinions; evaluations of disclosure letters; disclosure interviews with inventors and counsel; preparation, filing, and prosecution of patent applications relating to: silicon polymer chemistry and embodiments covering hard-coatings; adhesives, non-stick coatings, silicone elastomers; production of hyperpure silicon; epoxy resins and curing agents; fiber resin matrix prepegs and composites; emulsion-based paints and coatings; ultraviolet light screening agents; high-temperature lubricants; thermoplastics; secondary oil recovery and transmission of liquid media; highway construction; refractory composites; steam generators; Examiner interviews; preparation of appeal briefs; oral argument before the Board of Appeals; preparation and prosecution of reissue applications. Responsible for preparation and prosecution of trademark applications, trademark appeals and oral argument before the TTAB, and trademark oppositions. Responsible for all pretrial aspects of patent and trademark litigations. Prepare confidential disclosure agreements, perform legal research, and prepare legal memoranda.

1980-83   **MORAN, SULLIVAN, FORREST & YEE**
Provo, UT   ASSOCIATE ATTORNEY

Managed major aspects of patent prosecution and appeal, including: evaluation of disclosures; interviews with inventors and counsel; preparation, filing, and prosecution of patent applications relating to silicon hard coatings and vulcanites, treated silica fibers, thermoplastics, wire enamels, frangible adhesive containers, and patent litigation (including drafting and responding to interrogatories, examination and control of documents and exhibits, organizing depositions, legal research, and drafting legal memoranda).

-continued-

CHRONOLOGICAL

Resume Example #21 continued

1979-80   **HORVATH, SWEENEY & ARCHER**
              Salt Lake City, UT

              Conducted project to analyze terms of over 12,000 license agreements and enter-
              tainment contracts, and creation of data base allowing completion of same.

1972-77   **BRIGHAM YOUNG UNIVERSITY,** Department of Biochemistry
(summers)   Lab Assistant

              Supervised running of continuous, complex protein separation process; respon-
              sible for purifying, assaying, and storing selected enzymes; developed mutant
              strains of *Pseudomonas* bacteria; maintained and harvested several bacteria
              cultures.

EDUCATION   J.D. 1979   **BRIGHAM YOUNG UNIVERSITY**
                                       Equitas (BYLS newspaper) writer, summer intern
                                       in City Council President's Office

              B.A. Biological Sciences **BRIGHAM YOUNG UNIVERSITY**
              B.A. Psychology   Microbiology,
              1976   Physiological Psychology

ADMISSIONS   United States Patent and Trademark Office
              Bar of the State of Utah

MEMBERSHIPS   American Bar Association
              Copyright Society of the U.S.A.   RELEVANT AND
              Utah Patent, Trademark, and Copyright Law Association   NECESSARY TO THE
              Utah County Lawyers' Association   LEGAL PROFESSION.

Resume Example #22: A homemaker with some earlier professional experience pulls it all together.

RAMONA REENTRY

1404 Marlboro
Minneapolis, MN 55401

Work (612) 555-0011
Home (612) 555-1100

OBJECTIVE: Journalism: Financial / Economic / General News Reporting.

> STRAIGHTFORWARD JOB OBJECTIVE.

SIGNIFICANT ACCOMPLISHMENTS:
- Initiated, organized, and successfully led PTA. Sponsored 1-year fund drive raising $86,250 (1989).
- Selected to 5-member Emment County Scholastic Achievement Board, which distributes $50,000 in college scholarships to deserving, under-privileged high school seniors.
- Successfully organized 44-member petitioning group, which led to tax referendum being placed on Emment County election — 1988.
- Chosen as one of four finalists for "Volunteer Citizen of the Year —1987.
- Regular contributor to the National Scholastic Achiever, a quarterly journal. Have published 11 articles from 1981 to present.

> CREATES A BUSY, EFFICIENT IMPRESSION OF SOMEONE WHO GETS THINGS DONE.

> NOTEWORTHY.

EDUCATION:
- B.S. Journalism: University of Chicago, 1981. 3.4/4.0 GPA; graduated "with distinction."
- Post-graduate study: Illinois State University, 1985-1987. Economics and Finance — 8 classes at senior undergraduate level. 3.9/4.0 GPA.

> DEMONSTRATES CONTINUATION OF ACTIVE INTERESTS.

PROFESSIONAL EXPERIENCE:

National Scholastic Achiever, 1987 - Present;
Part-time (20 hrs./wk.) position — research, writing, and office management.

Chicago Tribune, 1981 - 1983;
Special Events Reporter. Left voluntarily to raise family.

Excellent references available upon request.

> O.K. TO INCLUDE FOR SOMEONE NOT CURRENTLY EMPLOYED.

FUNCTIONAL

81

Resume Example #23: A graduating senior with very little work experience searches for his first job.

RALPH T. RAWFELLOW

137 St. Clair Avenue
Hamilton, New York 13346
(315) 404-1138

STRAIGHTFORWARD AND REASONABLE JOB (NOT CAREER) OBJECTIVE.

OBJECTIVE   An entry-level computer programming position leading to program design.

EDUCATION   Colgate University, Hamilton, New York
B.S. in Electrical Engineering, with a minor in Computer Programming and Design, to be completed in June 1991 (3.4/4.0 grade average).

EMPHASIS ON ACADEMIC CREDITS IN LIEU OF JOB EXPERIENCE.

IMPORTANT.

EMPLOYMENT EXPERIENCE

Summer 1990: Business Machines International, Syracuse, New York. Operated IBM 3081 and 3033 mainframes. Knowledge in a wide range of software applications.

Summer 1989: Radio Hut, Syracuse, New York. Sold home computers and video games. Selected as Employee of the Month, August 1989.

LIMITED, BUT WELL-STATED WORK EXPERIENCE.

SPECIAL SKILLS

ESSENTIAL INFORMATION.

* Familiarity with OS/COBOL, BAL, FORTRAN, BASIC, and Assembly.

* Working knowledge of IBM 3081 and 3083 mainframes running under OS/MVS/TSO using CICS and IMS.

SIGNIFICANT ACCOMPLISHMENTS

* Helped set up program to increase accuracy and speed of compiling and recording student grade averages.

* Published (with Dr. L.B. Bollo) two papers in "Programming News."

OTHERWISE NOT VERY BELIEVABLE.

* Developed software program entitled "Finacom"; makes spreadsheet organization easier and faster.

* Dean's list member 6 of 7 semesters thus far completed.

MAKES THE MOST OUT OF VERY LITTLE.

FUNCTIONAL

Resume Example #24: Career enhancement on the middle-management level.

MANLY R. UPBOUND

12 Arcadia Drive
El Paso, Texas 79901

Telephone: (512) 555-6543 (Res.)
(512) 555-1111 (Bus.)

CAREER OBJECTIVE: To direct a dynamic, ambitious (small or medium-sized) electronics corporation, and to help it grow into a major industry player.

EMPLOYMENT:
1982 to
Present

[SPECIFIC AND AMBITIOUS.]

P. Reynolds Corporation. El Paso, Texas — Director of Research and Development. Responsible for new product development and testing from innovation through feasibility. Includes management of a staff of 23.

[GOOD BALANCE BETWEEN HISTORY AND ACCOMPLISHMENTS.]

* **Recruited** and developed research team of 12 engineers within first 18 months on job. No turnover on staff to date.

* **Developed** methodology of counter redesign of electronic sensing devices. This saved corporation $400,000 in first year of implementation.   [DOLLAR SAVINGS.]

* **Managed** R&D team responsible for major design changes to production facility resulting in 30% labor savings.

Laboratory Testing Corporation. Little Rock. Arkansas — Senior Research Supervisor. Headed up 8-person product testing group responsible for establishing performance specifications.

* **Initiated** group performance standards, which allowed for "on-time" completion standard of 92%. Prior group had maintained 55% standard.   [MEASURABLE IMPROVEMENT.]

* **Created** test procedures that revealed product design errors, saving client manufacturers over $2 million during four years in this position.

Research Analyst. Member of a new tooling group developing and testing newly installed manufacturing lines involving high-usage, electronically-controlled feeder and assembly units.

[SHOWS INITIATIVE.]

* **Supervised** 4-person group that blueprinted wiring schematics for entire final production assembly line for Volkswagen of America. Used computer line tracking design of our own making (first time used within automotive industry).

* **Promoted** to group supervisor (youngest supervisor of research group in corporation).

EDUCATION: University of Texas at El Paso, BS and MSEE 1977. Completed graduate work with a 4.8 GPA out of possible 5.0.

AWARDS: American Society of Electrical Engineers — "Research Engineer of the Year," 1982. Received recognition for usage of voltage conductors in high-use assembly units.

[RELEVANT AWARD.]

[THIS RESUME SAYS A GREAT DEAL IN A RELATIVELY SMALL SPACE.]

CHRONOLOGICAL

Resume Example #25: Fast-track creativity seeking career enhancement.

RITA I. FANTASIA

90 Treefilled Lane
Hillsboro, Oregon 97123

Telephone: Home (503) 555-5252
Office (503) 555-2525

Employment:

1983-Present
VENUS BEAUTY PRODUCTS, Portland, Oregon
Major beauty products supply distributor and retailer, annual sales of $30 million.

Proprietary Market Manager
Responsibilities:
* Buyer of 40 proprietary line items for 38 distribution centers nationwide.
* Annual open to buy budget: $8 million
* Product and package planning, design, and development.
* Market analysis and research.
* Sales forecasting and evaluation of new and existing products.
* Advertising and promotion including introductory offers and deals, quarterly catalogue, and monthly news articles.

> UNUSUAL FORMAT SUCCESSFULLY DEMONSTRATES WHAT SHE WAS SUPPOSED TO DO, AND WHAT SHE DID.

> RESPONSIBLE.

> CREATIVITY.

Achievements:
* Established annual budget for new product development.
* Initiated seven new products from planning to point of purchase within ten months.
* Designed and authored a training manual for sales staff.
* Presented several slide presentations for training sessions.

> LOOK AT HOW MUCH INFORMATION IS CONTAINED IN ONLY FIFTEEN WORDS.

1981-1983
DEVON INCORPORATED, New York, New York

Account Manager
Responsibilities:
* Sales of cosmetic line through three levels of distribution: manufacturer to distributor, retailer, and consumer.
* Traveled 34 states with average annual sales of $2.3 million.
* Conducted sales training meetings, seminars, and workshops for distributors and retailers.
* Created and designed displays, exhibits, and promotional materials for trade shows.

> SPECIFIC FIGURES ENHANCE CREDIBILITY.

Achievements:
* Selected by Devon administrators to open select new markets with distributors and retailers in 22 states.
* Designed, complete with layout and copy, photo-ready "Devon Advertising Kit."
* Implemented new product promotion, including product, display, and promotional material.

> ACTION STATEMENTS REVEAL THE FULL RANGE OF ACCOMPLISHMENTS IN A MEANINGFUL CONTEXT.

-continued-

> BEAUTIFULLY ORGANIZED AND IMPRESSIVE.

CHRONOLOGICAL

Resume Example #25 continued

RITA I. FANTASIA

Awards:
* Devon Sales of the Month Award (9 times).
* Best Sales Presentation Award (1981, 1986, 1988).

> THE TYPE OF AWARD THAT GETS ATTENTION.

1978-1981
MANNEQUIN MODEL AGENCY, St. Claire Shores, Michigan
Licensed fashion and modeling school and agency.
<u>Director of Education</u>

Responsibilities:
* Researched, designed, and authored three curriculum programs.
* Designed and authored training manual.
* Trained, managed, and supervised office and teaching staff.
* Coordinated and conducted nearly 100 seminars and lectures to civic, education, and business groups.

EDUCATION: 1974 OREGON COLLEGE, Medford, Oregon
B.S., Fashion Merchandising and Marketing.

> SOLID ACADEMIC CREDENTIALS.

FOREIGN
LANGUAGES: French, Spanish.

> NO PERSONAL DETAILS ABOUT MARITAL OR FAMILY STATUS.

Resume Example #26: A retired executive seeking part-time consulting work.

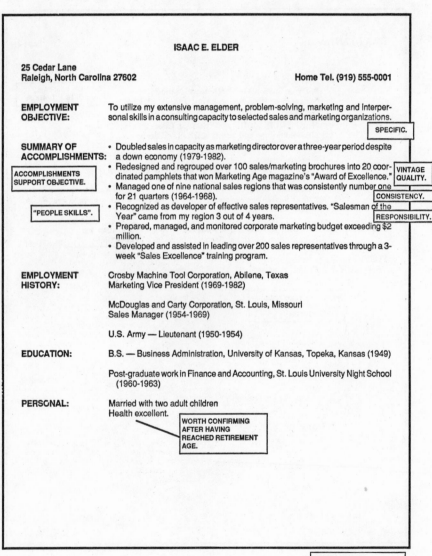

ISAAC E. ELDER

25 Cedar Lane
Raleigh, North Carolina 27602   Home Tel. (919) 555-0001

EMPLOYMENT OBJECTIVE:
To utilize my extensive management, problem-solving, marketing and interpersonal skills in a consulting capacity to selected sales and marketing organizations.

> SPECIFIC.

SUMMARY OF ACCOMPLISHMENTS:
- Doubled sales in capacity as marketing director over a three-year period despite a down economy (1979-1982).
- Redesigned and regrouped over 100 sales/marketing brochures into 20 coordinated pamphlets that won Marketing Age magazine's "Award of Excellence."
- Managed one of nine national sales regions that was consistently number one for 21 quarters (1964-1968).
- Recognized as developer of effective sales representatives. "Salesman of the Year" came from my region 3 out of 4 years.
- Prepared, managed, and monitored corporate marketing budget exceeding $2 million.
- Developed and assisted in leading over 200 sales representatives through a 3-week "Sales Excellence" training program.

> ACCOMPLISHMENTS SUPPORT OBJECTIVE.

> "PEOPLE SKILLS".

> VINTAGE QUALITY.

> CONSISTENCY.

> RESPONSIBILITY.

EMPLOYMENT HISTORY:
Crosby Machine Tool Corporation, Abilene, Texas
Marketing Vice President (1969-1982)

McDouglas and Carty Corporation, St. Louis, Missouri
Sales Manager (1954-1969)

U.S. Army — Lieutenant (1950-1954)

EDUCATION:
B.S. — Business Administration, University of Kansas, Topeka, Kansas (1949)

Post-graduate work in Finance and Accounting, St. Louis University Night School (1960-1963)

PERSONAL:
Married with two adult children
Health excellent.

> WORTH CONFIRMING AFTER HAVING REACHED RETIREMENT AGE.

> FITTING A LONG, SUCCESSFUL CAREER ONTO A BRIEF BUT POWERFUL PAGE.

COMBINED

Resume Example #27: A high-tech entrepreneur employs a creative two-column technique to show individual but concurrent activities.

SIGMUND R. TIMEWINDER

9009 N St. NW
Washington, DC 20036

Office (202) 555-7777
Home (202) 555-1111

SUMMARY:
Over 25 years of professional *management* and *technical* achievements.

> BROAD-BASED
> TECHNICAL AND
> EDUCATIONAL SKILLS.

MANAGEMENT
1982-Present
President, Data Software Innovations Group, Ltd. Responsible for budgeting, planning, equipment acquisition, hiring outside services (legal, accounting, etc.), marketing and production. DATASIG has changed work patterns and demonstrably improved productivity of such major client software development organizations as Ball Labs, Ballcore, and other major corporations.

1978-80
Systems Engineering Manager, Business Machines International (Banking Office). Managed two teams of Systems Engineers, including technical specialists (IMS, CICS, MVS, SNA, Project Management). Planned branch office technical staffing and training. Interviewed and hired for my own unit. Recognized each year as one of top 10% of Systems Engineering managers.

1975-76
Project Manager, Business Machines International (Financial Office). Designed and managed implementation of major teleprocessing network, which included the first SNA-distributed processors shipped in company history. Planned project and quality control, devised new techniques for programming, testing, user training, and physical planning. Established program of "walkthroughs" to assure quality of system. This 250 staff-month project was delivered on time. Network and methods developed by me were adopted company-wide as models for development of similar networks.

> BOTTOM-LINE
> RESPONSIBILITY.

-continued-

TECHNICAL
1988-Present
Consultant to Port Authority and Transit Authority of New York. Designed, developed, and taught courses in personnel administration and inventory concepts.

1986-88
Consultant to Ball Communications Research. Designed and developed business model and architecture for large distributed data base.

1985-Present
Consultant to N&WG. Developed and taught courses n technical management, project planning, testing, and Q.A. Established Q.A. organization. Defined development metnodologies and tools for corporate standards.

1982-Present
Consultant to Ball Laboratories. Directed and implemented research and effective transfer of software engineering techniques to over 40 development projects. Measured results include 30% reduction in project development time, and 80% reduction in error rates.

1980-82
Senior Instructor, Business Machines International Systems Science Institute. Designed and taught management and software engineering courses to senior data processing management and staff of major customers.

1978-80
Adjunct Professor, Graduate School of Business, Fairleigh Dickenson University. Taught MBA program courses: Managing Data Processing (for D.P. professionals) and Information Systems (for non-D.P. executives).

-continued-

CHRONOLOGICAL

Resume Example #27 continued

MANAGEMENT continued

1971-74
Marketing Representative, Business Machines International (Financial Office). Achieved over 100% of quota each year.

1962-64
1st. Lt., US Army. In charge of Signal Corps communications repair facility in France. Managed 35 civilian and enlisted personnel. Instituted new operating procedures that reduced number of deadlined items by 80%.

EDUCATION and HONORS
Business Machines International Management School
Business Machines International Systems Research
    Institute
University of Connecticut (mathematics major)
Cornell University (mathematics major)

M.A. degree in mathematics, 1962
B.S. degree (cum laude) in mathematics, 1960
Elected member of Sigma Xi, National Science Honorary Society
Elected member of M.A.A., Mathematical Association of America

> STRONG ACADEMIC CREDENTIALS.

TECHNICAL continued

1976-78
Regional Teleprocessing Specialist, Business Machines International, New York Regional Office. Reviewed communication proposals for technical accuracy and feasibility. Conducted courses in Communications Management, SNA, VTAM, and TCAM for employees and customers in metropolitan New York.

1974-76
Senior Systems Engineer, Business Machines International Financial Branch Office. Provided technical support for all facets of data processing, including hardware configuration, software generation, DB/DC design, programming, and operations.

1968-71
Staff Instructor, Business Machines International Advanced Education Center. Developed and taught O.S. internals courses.

1964-68
Systems Engineer, IBM New Haven Branch Office. Provided DOS support. Participated in Alpha test for first release of BTAM.

1960-62
Instructor, University of Connecticut Mathematics Department. Conducted undergraduate courses in Algebra and Finite Mathematics.

PROFESSIONAL AFFILIATIONS
    AMA, DPMA, IEEE, ACM, ICCA, ASM

> APPROPRIATE TO THE PROFESSION.

AVAILABLE HARDWARE
    IBM PC/AT with capability to network with UNIX host.

> SHOWS ABILITY TO WORK OFF-SITE.

PUBLICATIONS
    "Adding an End-of-File Marker," Exchange of IBM PC Information, July 1985

Resume Example #28: A recent graduate who is light on experience emphasizes qualities valued by employers.

MARGO LIGHTLY

22 Story Avenue
Lancaster, PA 28717

Home (606)555-1111
Messages (606)555-3333

EDUCATION

1990   B.A., Management, Rutgers University
         3.3/4.0 G.P.A., President's Academic List last 6 semesters

1986-88 Completed 16 hours of computer coursework covering desktop hardware/
         software; FORTRAN; Lotus 1-2-3 | SOLID SKILL. |

OBJECTIVE

To apply my management/organizational, computer and foreign language (French and German) skills to an international firm's operations and service delivery.

CAPABILITIES

| DESIRABLE TRAITS. |

* Proven track record in creatively using computers to organize work and paper flow

* Work well under pressure, willingly assisting peers and superiors in a teamwork environment

* Effectively helping to fulfill customer requirements and expectations for quality service

EXPERIENCE

| INITIATIVE AND RESPONSIBILITY. |

* Sold executive gift baskets in person and by phone at $1600 - $2200 per month

* Initiated and developed order tracking system for gift basket business substantially reducing order errors

* Named Employee of the Month (twice in 6 months)

1988 -   Sales Representative
 Present   The Executive Gift Store, Brunswick, N.J.

1987 (summer)   Assistant Manager,
                Fiona's Apparel, Princeton, N.J.

1986 (summer)   Hostess/Waitress,
                Henri's Cafe, Boston, MA

COMBINED

Resume Example #29: An unemployed professional looking for a new job.

JULIUS B. MOHAMMED
417 Lake Shore Drive
Evanston, Illinois 60201
312/555-5151

OBJECTIVE: To direct the art department of a progressive advertising agency or consumer products company where experience in creating innovative advertising programs, developing effective communications, and creating motivational programs is needed.

> THEY DON'T COME MUCH BETTER THAN THIS!

EXPERIENCE SUMMARY: 12 years of marketing-oriented experience including illustration and art design, photography, writing, creative product introduction, leadership, and problem-solving.

> GOOD LEAD-IN TO ACCOMPLISHMENT STATEMENTS.

CREATIVE PROGRAM: Conceptualized and headed up group that produced ad insert showing 4 new stereo receivers used within program at 1986 National Stereo Product Conference. Received 2 design awards.

> CREATIVITY.

INNOVATIVE PUBLICITY: Originated "Sound Advice" exhibit at National Stereo Manufacturers Exhibit in 1985. Exhibit rated #1 by exhibit participants. Written up in Advertising Age (June '85) article entitled "Innovations in Exhibit Design."

> ORGANIZATIONAL SKILLS.

PROFIT ENHANCER: Produced traveling video series showing dealers how new 1981 product innovations could enhance their sales of Concord stereo line. Sales increased 37% during 1982 following video series. Next highest sales increase year had been 23%.

> GIVES PERSPECTIVE TO NUMERICALLY STATED ACHIEVEMENT.

ADEPT MANAGER: Reduced overall marketing/advertising budget by 26% through consolidation of outside work, increasing quality of brochures, reducing quantities of piecemeal promotional materials: resulted in 24% sales increase.

> EMPHASIZES MANAGEMENT SKILLS.

EDUCATION: Diploma in Creative Design — Center for Creative Studies, University of Chicago, 1973.

AWARDS: National Stereo Manufacturers Association — Two first-place awards for exhibit design excellence. National Association of Exhibit Designers: 1988 award for Creative Design of the Year.

> RELEVANT AWARDS.

PUBLICATIONS: Contributor to Exhibitors Journal.

> DRAWS ATTENTION AWAY FROM QUESTION OF UNEMPLOYMENT IN A POSITIVE MANNER.

FUNCTIONAL

Resume Example #30: Careful organization solves the problem of squeezing a lot of information onto two pages.

ARTHUR D. ROSENBERG

250 Palisades Parkway
Cliffside Park, N.J. 07010

Home: 201/555-0000
Office: 210/555-0000

SUMMARY: Over 20 years of professional accomplishments.

THIS LETS US KNOW
WHAT IS TO FOLLOW.

WRITER/EDITOR	MANAGER/INSTRUCTOR
Technical	Training
Instructional	Administration
Advertising/Promotion	Marketing/Sales

SPECIAL SKILLS: Solving problems; transforming incomplete or confusing technical and instructional materials into accurate, readable documentation.

STRONG, CONFIDENT
STATEMENT.

SOFTWARE: Multimate, WordStar, DW2, Lotus 1-2-3, Flow Charting, OLM (IDMS), TSO/ICCF/SPF/IBM System 38 editors.

ACHIEVEMENTS:

WRITER

GOOD ACTION WORDS
AND STATEMENTS.

* Project Leader of group creating systems and user documentation for IDMS order processing, accounts receivable, inventory control, and customer/product/warehouse/data base/security maintenance systems.
* Documented major IDMS transportation system, including user guides and instructional manuals; conducted training programs for instructors.
* Catalogued over 4000 systems-produced reports.
* Provided PC support and training; evaluated desktop publishing software and applications.
* Developed HELP screens for brokerage system on IBM 38.
* Documented implementation of payroll/personnel software system, including functional specs and user manuals.
* Researched and wrote bank procedures on security systems and data collection/compilation for hardware/software productivity reports.
* Created technical/instructional documentation for IMS (IBM-compatible) payroll/personnel system.
* Researched and wrote two published consumer-oriented studies on computer-based energy management systems.

EDITOR

* Editor, "The Consultants Interface," the monthly newsletter of the New York/New Jersey Chapter of the ICCA (Independent Computer Consultants Association).
* Published college math and business textbooks.
* Translated foreign language technical and promotional documentation for Grenoble Winter Olympics.
* Edited user/technical documentation, instructional manuals, annual reports, catalogs, proposals.

-continued-

THE INITIAL DRAFT OF THIS
RESUME COVERED 8-1/2 PAGES.
IT TOOK A LOT OF IMAGINATION AND
REFLECTION TO GET IT DOWN TO A
REASONABLE SIZE.

COMBINED

Resume Example #30 continued

ARTHUR D. ROSENBERG   Page 2

MANAGER   * Established New York office for human resources firm.
                 * Supervised multinational staff at U.N. agency in Geneva.
                 * Directed marketing activities for two international publishers of technical/educa-
                   tional materials.

INSTRUCTOR   * Conducted classes and seminars at the following:
                     John Wiley & Sons   Union College (N.J.)
                     Purolator-Courier   University of Stockholm (Sweden)
                     McGraw-Hill   Berlitz School (Paris)

EMPLOYMENT HISTORY   ┌──────────────────────┐
1979 -   │ SUGGESTS THAT THERE │
Present   Independent Consultant   │ WERE EVEN MORE.   │
                                                          └──────────────────────┘
                                                 TECHNICAL WRITER,
                                                 SYSTEMS ANALYST, TRAINER

Recent Clients:

                 John Wiley & Sons   Marsh & McLennan
                 Purolator Courier   U.S. Department of Education
                 McGraw-Hill   Paladyne Software Systems
                 Paramount Pictures   Information Science
                 Morgan Guaranty   Comerica-Detroit Bank
                 RAVA Systems   Delmar Publishers
                 Marine Computer
                 Port Authority/NY-NJ

1975-   International Labor Office   ASSISTANT MANAGER,
1979   Geneva, Switzerland   PUBLICATIONS

1973-   Dun Donnelly Publishing   EDITOR: BUSINESS
1975   New York   & MATHEMATICS

1972-   Harcourt Brace Jovanovich   ASSISTANT MANAGER,
1973   New York   PUBLICATIONS

1968-   McGraw-Hill Book Company   MARKETING MANAGER
1972   New York

PROFESSIONAL   ICCA — Independent Computer Consultants Association   ┌──────────────┐
ASSOCIATIONS   The Authors Guild   │ RELEVANT   │
                 The Authors League   │ AFFILIATIONS.│
                                                                        └──────────────┘

EDUCATION   M.A., English, French — University of Grenoble, France
                 B.A., Psychology — University of California at Los Angeles

FOREIGN
LANGUAGES   French, Spanish, German, Italian, Dutch, Swedish

92

We're confident these widely divergent resumes have provided you with a format and some fresh ideas that will enable you to display your skills effectively. They will encourage the interviewer to spend more time studying your resume, and less time looking at the 244 others.

The successful resume can be thought of as an art form. We don't want you to think of your resume as a potential minefield, where the slightest "mistake" can eliminate you from the running. As these resume demonstrate, there are countless ways to present your background in its most favorable light; there is, of course, no single right way. Follow the format in any of these resumes, or borrow from several; the choice is yours.

Now that you've seen some of the recommended methods, a look at some of the wrong ways of writing resumes may prove instructive (and, perhaps, entertaining).

Chapter Five:
The 5 Worst Resumes We've Ever Seen

If a good resume is a work of art, a bad resume can be a masterpiece of self-destruction.

Included in this chapter are five of the worst resumes we've ever seen, selected from among those which we assume to have been honest (if misguided) attempts at interesting a potential employer. That they fail is obvious. We shall briefly point out some of their most poignant flaws, and how three of them could have been successfully rewritten.

RESUME   VINCENT VAGUELY

PERSONAL: Birth Date: February 25, 1963. Single. Excellent
                health. Willing to travel and/or relocate.

EDUCATION: B.S. in Business Administration, Central Michigan
                University, with a major in finance, 24 credit hours;
                additional concentration in marketing and economics.
                Overall GPA 3.1. Date of graduation, May 7, 1985.

EXTRA-   Marketing Association, 1983, 1984, 1985.
CURRICULAR   Finance Club, 1984-85.
ACTIVITIES: Student Advisory Council, 1984-85.
                Theta Chi Fraternity - Secretary, 1983-1984
                    Rush Chairman, 1984-85

INTERESTS,   Sports (golf, bowling, softball, basketball); leisure
HOBBIES: reading and music.

WORK   1981 - Warehouseman for Leaseway of Westland, MI
EXPERIENCE: 1982 - Warehouseman for Leaseway of Westland, MI
                1983 - Warehouseman for Leaseway of Westland, MI
                1984 - Temporary Welding Inspector - Ford Motor
                Company (after being laid off, painted exteriors of
                homes).

ADDRESS: Home: 66666 Fox Glen
                Farmington Hills, MI 48018
                Phone: 313-666-0606, 313-666-0607

COMMENTS: I feel that I am a dependable, personable and hard
                working individual who could be an asset to your
                business.

NAME: VINCENT VAGUELY

Vincent Vaguely's vitae could (and maybe should) have been written on a 3 × 5 index card. This is the ideal size for recipes and other nonessentials. For although Vaguely feels he'd be an asset to our business, he has given us precious little data to support this optimistic view.

Now let's tear apart what Vincent Vaguely *did* include:

- *Resume:* Indeed, we know what it was intended to be, and so the label is superfluous.

- *Personal:* This information is unnecessary. If the writer insists on including it, he should have placed it at the very end.

- *Education:* Adequate, but poorly presented.

- *Extra-Curricular Activities:* Okay, but "Related Activities" might sound more grown-up.

- *Interests, Hobbies:* Who cares?

- *Work Experience:* Should list the last job first. The same job need not be listed more than once. No mention is made of job responsibilities or accomplishments.

- *Address:* We finally discover where Vincent Vaguely lives. Of course, the address belongs up at the top.

- *Comments:* Unsubstantiated and unconvincing.

□ □ □

```
CHARLES "CHUCK" CONFUSER            Telex:  Smartashell
Easy Street
Big Town, NJ   07990

Statement of Position
As of July 20, 1989

"U" are current unit valuations of relative worth to investor.

ASSETS
CURRENT ASSETS
Abilities Derived Through Current Major Classes
    Technical Capabilities              U  55
    Spirit of competition
    (less allowance for cooperation)        90
    Communicative capacity                  90
    Background in business courses         100
    Units from current major classes       335
    Leadership/Decision Making Ability     125
        TOTAL CURRENT ASSETS               460
Health and Physical Attributes             100
Former Education                            75
Determination, Self-Confidence,
  and Self-Support (net of realization
  of dependence on others)                 125
Goodwill and Intangibles                   100
TOTAL ASSETS                            U 860


LIABILITIES AND STOCKHOLDERS EQUITY
CURRENT LIABILITIES
Amount Due Others for Maintenance
  of Interest and Self-Development      U 235
    Amount Due Work Experience             115
    TOTAL CURRENT LIABILITIES             350
Long Term Debt to
  Supporters of Current Position          140
Debt related to Mark 12:17                110
TOTAL LIABILITIES                         600
STOCKHOLDERS EQUITY
Common Stock                               55
Retained Earnings
  (to facilitate future development)       210
TOTAL LIABILITIES
AND STOCKHOLDERS EQUITY                 U 860
```

NAME: CHARLES "CHUCK" CONFUSER

Believe it or not, such resumes as this actually *do* turn up from time to time. Chuck has obviously confused numerical facility with imagination and cleverness. A potential employer would not. This is not to say that innovation and creativity are negative ingredients in resume-writing perforce. But they must be applied judiciously and intelligently so as to complement, not dominate, important and clearly-organized information.

This document not only is *not* a resume, it doesn't come close to fulfilling the *purpose* of a resume. Even if someone took the trouble to try and figure out the "formula" (bear in mind the other 244 resumes waiting on the interviewer's desk), it provides no comprehensible basis on which to evaluate the aspirant's experience or abilities.

The lesson here is that a resume should provide its readers with relevant information; it shouldn't test their patience.

And as if all of this were not enough, the use of a nickname is another "no-no".

Eleanora Unsura
1404 Moore Ave.
Lincoln, MO   65438
(417) 555-1174
Social Sec. No. 390-92-6649

Level of Education:
High School Harper Woods High School 4 years
Business School Hallmark Business Machines Institute 9 months
Course of study Computer Programming
Specialization Cobol & RPGII Languages
Career Objective To Work Hard and become a good Programmer
Possible Salary $10,000 to $20,000 a year
Employment Experience:
Present Employer Whall Security Corp.
Job Title Security Officer.
Date of Employment 12/27/82. Current Salary $4.24 an hour
Job Responsibility To Take care of clients property from Fire or Theft.
Previous Employer Little Caecars Inc.
Job Title Store manager & pizza maker
Dates of Employment March, 1982 to November, 1982 Salary $180 a week.
Job Responsibility To make pizzas when busy and to do daily paper work.
Personal References: Billy and Jane Smith, 1403 Moore Ave. (across the street).

Truly Yours

Eleanora Unsura

Eleanora Unsura

NAME: ELEANORA UNSURA

What's wrong with this little monstrosity? Almost everything, alas. The major flaws are that it is grammatically abhorrent, poorly punctuated, full of misspellings, and unpleasing to the eye. It goes on to flout, destroy, or merely ignore the fundamental rules of writing a successful resume.

To mention just a few specifics, salaries (past, present, and requested) should *never* appear upon a resume. Nor should references, or jobs like "pizza maker." If you insist on such references, at least spell the name of your employer correctly. Finally, Eleanora's resume doesn't give the interviewer a chance to think about her background. There is no open space, relevancies and irrelevancies are intermingled, and it is completely lacking in structure.

Ms. Unsura gives us no idea of what she may have to offer a potential employer. She would be well-advised to solicit help in organizing and writing a resume with purpose and technique!

On the following page, we offer an alternative:

ELEANORA UNSURA

1404 Moore Avenue   417/555-1174
Lincoln, Missouri 65338

OBJECTIVE: A programming position allowing for professional
                    skill development, multiple applications, and
                    potential for career growth.

EMPLOYMENT   Whall Security Corporation - Security Officer
HISTORY: Provide security service to a variety of business
1982 - Present   clients - hospitals to manufacturing concerns.

                    *Uncovered electrical fire in early stages while
                     on patrol at Parkcrest Hospital, resulting in
                     quick and easy smothering of fire and saving
                     potential loss of costly research equipment.

                    *Maintained perfect attendance record while
                     employed at Whall, despite working at least 30+
                     hours/week and completing coursework at
                     Hallmark.

                    *"Employee of the Month" - Recipient 7 times.

1982   Little Caesar's Incorporated - Store Manager
                    Managed $515,000 annual receipt, 7-employee
                    carry-out restaurant.

                    *Reduced losses from incorrectly filled orders
                     by redesigning order form. This resulted in a
                     55% drop in losses.

                    *Appointed manager at age 17 and while still a
                     senior in high school.

EDUCATION: Hallmark Business Machine Institute - 1986.
                    Completed 9-month program with a proficiency
                    score on final testing of 92%.

                    Cape Harris H.S., 1982. Graduated within College
                    Preparatory Curriculum.

ACTIVE   Home computers, computer technical journals.
INTERESTS:

It's difficult to believe, but this is the same Eleanora Unsura who authored the previous interviewer's nightmare. With some careful thought given to her achievements, a newfound respect for the English language, some carefully-chosen action verbs, and a format designed to save the potential interviewer from a headache, Eleanora's resume has made a Pygmalion-like transition.

```
                              RESUME
I.M. Brusk                              Department of Geography
123 S. Adams                          California State University
Correl, California  91106               80 State College Avenue
(213) 000-0000                        Fullerton, California  91106
                                               (213) 000-0001

EDUCATION

1983 - present  School of Business Administration & Economics
                California State University-Fullerton  M.B.A.

1972 - 1976     Economic Geography Option
                U.C. Berkeley    Ph.D.

1969 - 1972     Geography, Major - Economics, Minor   B.A.
                University of Bristol (England)   Special Honors

WORK EXPERIENCE

1980 - present  Associate Professor
                Department of Geography
                California State University-Fullerton

1976 - 1980     Assistant Professor
                Department of Geography
                California State University-Fullerton

1975 - 1976     Instructor
                Department of Economics
                University of San Francisco

CONSULTING

1982 - 1988     Urban Econometrics Co., Fullerton, Ca.

1982 - 1985     Market Profiles, Inc., Tustin, Ca.

1982            Orange County Forecast and Analysis Center

AWARDS, HONORS

1973 - 1974     James P. Sutton Fellowship, U.C. Berkeley

1972-1973

                Thomas and Elizabeth Williams Scholarship,
                Glamorgan City Council

1969 - 1972     Special Honors, University of Bristol
```

NAME: BRUSK, I.M.

What a pity to have amassed such an impressive record of academic excellence and to portray it in such an unimpressive fashion.

This resume tells us that I.M. Brusk has earned an MBA, a PhD, and special honors. We can further deduce, with careful study, that the individual was promoted from Assistant to Associate Professor.

The rest is speculation. Has this apparently intelligent person published? What courses and seminars has he taught? What are his academic and scientific specialties? What was the nature of his consulting? Has he any noteworthy research in progress? What, if any, are his goals? Why, we don't even know if he is, in fact, a *he* or a *she*.

Presumably, Professor Brusk is looking for a highly specialized position. But there are other qualified people out there with PhDs and honors of their own in competition. Given similar academic credentials, those whose resumes present them in a more interesting light are likelier to get the interview.

Our advice to I.M. Brusk is to rewrite this resume with the elements we've outlined in *The Resume Handbook*. It might look something like the one on the next page.

ISABELLA M. BRUSK

123 South Adams   Residence: 213/000-0000
Correl, California 91106   Work: 213/000-0000

EXPERIENCE California State University - Fullerton, Associate Professor, Department of
1976 -   Geography. Responsible for curriculum development for entire
Current   department covering 3,700 students annually. Personally direct 10
            department classes each year, including newly-designed class entitled
            "Changing Weather Patterns - Dawn of a New Age."

            ● Co-authored "Economic Cycle Influences of Changing Political
              Boundaries", a highly-acclaimed series of articles appearing in July-
              October 1988 issues of the Research Economist.

            Selected as:

            ● Member of Governor's Council on Earthquake Readiness, a 16-member
              task force of business, academic and government people assessing
              current state readiness regarding safety, economic disruption and
              proposed construction considerations. Youngest member of panel.

            ● Rated 96.4 out of 100 by nearly 750 students attending my classes
              during 1976-88. "90" is considered "outstanding."

            ● Developed and tested computer model identifying economic trends (i.e.,
              unemployment rates, median incomes, others) caused by changing
              populations. This was accomplished during a consulting assignment
              with Urban Econometrics, Fullerton, CA.

            ● Conceived, designed and sold predictive voting model that pinpoints
              political voting trends utilizing demographics rather than polling. This
              predictive model has accurately predicted 27 out of 29 county races in
              1983-86.

1975-1976   University of San Francisco, Instructor - Department of Economics.
            Responsible for leading one senior-level undergrad and two graduate-
            level Microeconomics classes involving 120+ students.

            ● Developed instructional curriculum for 60-hour class entitled "Economic
              Patterns and Their Historical Perspectives."

108

page 2

PROFESSIONAL ASSOCIATION
American Association of Geographers

LANGUAGES
Welsh, French

PUBLICATIONS
1. Hydrological Implications of Geothermal Developments in the Imperial Valley of Southern California
   G. George, R.H. Foster, and D.K. Todd
   Sea Water Conversion Laboratory, UCB, Richmond, November, 1975.

2. 1978 Population Estimates
   G. George and G. Britton
   Report on the Status of Orange County, 1978.   Working Document No. 1, Forecast and Analysis Center, Orange County, CA.

3. The Frequency of Social Contracts within a Time-Space Framework.
   G. George
   Submitted for publication.

PROFESSIONAL PAPERS

1. Intra-urban Interaction and Time-Space Budgets.
   G. George, D. Shimarua, and P. Barry
   Association of American Geographers, New Orleans, 1982.

2. The Soviet Concept of Optimal City Size
   G. George and C. Zumbrunnen
   Association of American Geographers, New Orleans, 1982.

EDUCATION

- Ph.D.-University of California at Berkeley, 1976.
  Economic Geography Option
- M.B.A.-California State University-Fullerton, 1966.
- B.A.-University of Bristol (England), 1972.
  Geography Major; Economics Minor.   Graduated with honors.

We now know not only that Dr. Brusk is a she, but we've also gained a wealth of important information omitted from her initial resume. We've learned about her areas of expertise, that she has published extensively, and that she's popular with her students. Dr. Brusk, we find, has been appointed to a government panel; she is familiar with state-of-the-art techniques (computer modeling), and has had consulting positions with private firms (no "bookish academic," this Dr. Brusk). Without any exaggeration, she has turned a limp and lifeless resume into one that will demand its share of recognition in a fiercely competitive market.

```
                              RESUME
                                OF
                         BART BRAMBLEBUSH

RESIDENCE:                              OFFICE:
808 Hopkins Drive East                  Graduate School of
Windsor, Ontario                           Business
                                           Administration
                                        The University of Windsor
                                        Windsor, Ontario


PROFESSIONAL EXPERIENCE:

        1980       The University of Windsor
        to         Windsor, Ontario
        Present
                   1986            Director of Placement
                   to              Graduate School of Business
                   Present         Administration

                   1984            Director, BBA Internship Program
                   to              Dearborn, Michigan Campus
                   1986
        1978       Substitute Teacher
        to         Windsor Public Schools
        1980       Windsor, Ontario

        1973       Training Manager
        to         Hespin & Marquette
        1977       Windsor, Ontario

        1970       Home Economics Teacher
        to         Weaton Public Schools
        1973       Weaton, Ontario

EDUCATION:
University of Windsor, Windsor, Ontario; Master of Business
Administration, 1982. Major: Industrial Relations

University of Buffalo, Buffalo, New York; Bachelor of Science,
1966. Major: Secondary Education

EXCELLENT REFERENCES AVAILABLE UPON REQUEST
```

NAME: BART BRAMBLEBUSH

The preceding resume is probably the most frequent, and thus typical, form of resume failure we've encountered. At first glance, it may not seem so bad. In fact, you may be saying, "Gee, that looks like mine!"

Indeed, Bramblebush's offering is not as obviously awful as some of the preceding examples of bad resumes. Its failure is more subtle and insidious, which is why we consider it more dangerous than the others. The problem isn't what we see, but rather what we don't.

At second glance, this sad excuse for a resume might be better suited to the epitaph etched in stone above his bones once Bart's career is terminated — it offers little more than the stuff of which memories are made. What — if anything — has Bart accomplished in his profession? Has he met with any noteworthy success? There must be *something* he has done over the years to interest a potential employer, but we certainly can't find it underneath his name.

Other than where Bramblebush has been, and when, this document provides job titles, identifies itself as his resume, and gratuitously promises good references to anyone who might be interested. Fortunately, we know Bart well enough to help him out of his predicament, and so we took the time to rewrite his chrono-illogical attempt into a solid resume. This version follows. Read both versions, and ask yourself if they appear to describe the same person.

BARTHOLOMEW B. BRAMBLEBUSH

808 Hopkins Lane Drive   Residence (519) 101-0001
Windsor, Ontario 74R 01S   Business (519) 010-1000

PROFESSIONAL OBJECTIVE
        Attainment of a managerial level position as a Programs
        Director, Project Manager or Section Head within a major
        university where my array of administrative, analytic,
        planning and leadership skills can be fully utilized.

EDUCATION
        M.B.A., University of Windsor, Windsor, Ontario-1982.
        Concentration in Industrial Relations. B.A., University of
        Buffalo, Buffalo, New York-1970. Major in Secondary
        Education.

SIGNIFICANT EXPERIENCE
        MANAGERIAL - Successfully headed 12-member, $540,000 annual
        budget placement function; increased enrollments 1147 over
        last 4 years at a 9000-student university.

        SYSTEMS DEVELOPMENT - Conceptualized and implemented
        computerized records system projected to save $175,000 in
        administrative expenses over next 3 years.

        FUNDS DEVELOPMENT - During 2-year assignment as BBA
        Internship Program Director: established 359 successful
        corporate relationships totaling 577 students, resulting in
        additional bottom-line impact to university of $205,000.

        PROGRAM DESIGN - Originated and initiated Student
        Enrollment Campaign involving promotional literature,
        student contacts at high schools and junior colleges, and
        direct mail: resulted in increase in enrollment during
        1987 of 660 over 1986.

        TRAINING DESIGN - Designed Comprehensive Management Program
        affecting 275 individuals covering all phases of management
        from planning to controlling for major Canadian retailer.

        TEACHING EXCELLENCE - Runner up two years in row (1972-73)
        as Teacher of the Year in a school district with 150 high
        school teachers.

POSITIONS
        1980 - Present Director of Placement, University of
                        Windsor, Windsor, Ontario (1984-Present).

                        Director of BBA Internship Programs,
                        University of Windsor (1980-84).

        1978 - 1980   Substitute Teacher, Windsor Public Schools.

        1973 - 1977   Training Manager, Hespin & Marquette Ltd.,
                        Windsor, Ontario.

        1970 - 1973   Home Economics Teacher, Weaton Public
                        Schools, Weaton, Ontario.

Unlike Bart's first resume, his second shows that his flatly-stated job titles were accompanied by significant managerial, fiscal, teaching, and operational responsibilities. In the first resume, his job progression seems sketchy and undefined. The improved version informs us of a logical progression toward the position he is seeking. Bart's (Bartholomew's, rather) second resume is an interview-getter.

□ □ □

Without belaboring the point, even losing resumes can be transformed into winners. All you need are several hours of honest reflection (armed, of course, with your "resume tools"), an awareness of how your background can make you valuable to a potential employer, and a quick review of the basic resume guidelines outlined in chapter two. The rest is personal: choosing the format, typestyle, and layout that you feel best suits your background, while avoiding the pitfalls of poor resume writing.

Except for the brief final chapter on resume layout and design, this is our final word on successful resumes. The examples we have given you will hopefully provide the tools you need for your own, unique profile.

However, this is not the end of *The Resume Handbook*. In the following chapters, we will discuss design and layout, and then focus on the two essential resume companions: the cover letter, and the personal sales (or broadcast) letter.

Chapter Six:
Resume Design and Layout

It's no less important that your resume be pleasing to the eye than for it to clearly present the facts of your job history. People need to breathe while talking and vary their pitch, otherwise their words would quickly descend into a relentless monotone of meaningless syllables. Similarly, the interviewer or potential employer reading your resume needs time to let his or her eyes "breathe," a chance to pause and digest the achievements you're presenting.

This chapter will serve as a brief guide to structuring a resume that is physically appealing and complementary to your background.

The first thing to consider is the paper on which your resume (and accompanying cover letter, or solo personal sales letter) will be printed. An off-white paper stock may help your resume stand out in a pile, but beware of using pastels or darker colors, which look unprofessional. White standard business-sized stationery, of course, is always acceptable. Your resume should attract attention because of your carefully-worded achievements, not the paper you use.

As we cautioned earlier, try to limit your resume to a single page unless you have several years of experience and a diversity of noteworthy achievements. The interviewer will appreciate it.

The next thing to consider is the method you use to put your resume on paper. You have three basic choices: typesetting, typing, or word processing.

Modern photocomposition typesetting gives you the clearest, sharpest image of the three, offering a wide variety of typestyles and effects, including italics, bold letters, and justified margins. It is reproduced from photographic paper, the reason for its clarity. Typesetting is the preferred method, but it is also the most expensive.

If you have your resume typed, avoid models with cloth or nylon ribbons. Instead, be sure to have it done on an office-quality typewriter with a plastic (or carbon) ribbon. This can make an important difference in the way your resume appears.

We recommend word processors, which offer the most flexible approach. They can be modified easily and quickly, stored, and targeted to specific employers or job openings. Word processors have come a long way, and the major packages offer a wide variety of typefaces and styles in standard and proportional spacing. In fact, they're amazingly similar to typesetting. Word processing is a relatively inexpensive alternative, and this is what we use ourselves.

The next thing to consider is the choice of typeface. While you want your resume to stand out, you don't want it to compete with funeral or wedding announcements. Our advice is that you stick to a simple, clean typeface. There are, of course, thousands of typefaces to choose from. However, we believe that those like English, Times Roman, or Helvetica are best because of their simplicity of design and clarity to the eye.

Another pitfall to avoid is combining different typeface styles (i.e., Times Roman and Helvetica). On the other hand, those within the same typeface family may be combined to produce an attractive visual effect. For example, Times Roman typefaces can come in light, light italic, medium, medium italic, bold, bold italic, and several other nuances.

Having chosen your typeface, it's time to lay out your resume. During the design phase, bear in mind that open spaces make your resume easier to read. Thus you should avoid cramming your page(s) with heavy masses of print. For example, compare Eleanora Unsura's two resumes in chapter five.

Finally, a word about printing those 25, 50, or 100 copies of the resume. If you have it typed, find and use the best quality offset printing process available. If you use a word processor, print as many originals as you need on attractive, letter-quality paper. Never send off photocopies of your resume to a potential employer. Photocopies are okay for friends or even employment agencies, but not the person with whom you want to win an interview.

Another point is that the resume you mail may be photocopied by a personnel department, and subsequently passed along to other members of their firm. Copies made from copies can lose readability. In an emergency, some professionally-maintained office photocopiers may do a good job. We think it's better to avoid such emergencies by always having "perfect" copies of your resume on hand.

A final word: proofread your resume at every step in this process, whether it's typeset, typed, or generated from a word processor. Get a knowledgeable friend or colleague to help. Mistakes on resumes are embarrassing and unacceptable; they may prove disastrous. No matter how much you may have paid to have your resume created, you're the one who loses if it isn't right. So be meticulous — don't settle for less than the very best.

Chapter Seven:
Cover Letters

Now that your resume is a polished gem, at least half the battle has been waged. It's time to hone a tool that lends your resume direction and appeal. You need a cover letter. After all, the potential employer, opening hundreds of resumes and letters daily, isn't going to know what to do with just a lonely resume.

Writing effective cover letters is often underestimated in the overall scheme of seeking a new job. But cover letters can be the important key to the right doors.

Take the one on the following page, for instance:

February 18, 1990

Arthur C. Reese
President
Southwest Tooling Research, Inc.
200 Mountain View Blvd.
Santa Fe, NM 80801

Dear Mr. Reese:

Enclosed please find my resume. After you review it, I am sure you will find that I'm a worthwhile and capable professional engineer who deserves further attention.

My current situation no longer offers me the challenge and responsibility level I demand. Because of this, I feel it is time to seek out another opportunity.

If there is any interest in my capabilities, you can reach me at 417/555-4414. I'm positive you will find the time you spend analyzing my capabilities well worth your time.

Sincerely,

Ann Carmichael

Ann Carmichael

Would you go on to read the attached resume if you received hundreds of similar documents each week? We doubt it. The letter leaves a lot to be desired: it fails to include vital information, lacks a definite purpose, and simply doesn't entice the recipient to read more.

Effective cover letters convey a sense of purpose. They project an air of enthusiasm — regarding both the writer and the company for which the writer wants to work. And they demonstrate the writer's understanding of the company's goals, either by supporting or challenging them.

OBJECTIVES OF THE COVER LETTER

A well-written cover letter satisfies the following objectives:

- It offers the job seeker an opportunity to personalize and target the resume to a particular person;

- It allows the writer to direct particular attention to specific skills that may be important to the reader;

- It enables the applicant to clearly state why this organization is of interest to him or her;

- It opens the door for further communication and follow-through.

Let's examine each of these points in depth:

☐ *Personalization:* The personalized aspect of a cover letter is one of its major strengths. A resume, by its very nature, is impersonal. When mailed without a personalized cover letter, a resume may create the impression that the addressee is merely one of several random stops along the campaign trail.

Always address the cover letter to a specific individual within the target organization, preferably to the person who appears most likely to have decision-making authority for the position sought. Sales candidates should address the sales or marketing officer, while engineers are advised to approach the director of engineering. Any well-stocked library will have a variety of research aids such as trade journals, Standard & Poor's *Register of Corporations, Directors, and Executives,* Dun & Bradstreet's *Million Dollar Directory,* and many other research sources. Solid research results in a list of specific individuals within target organizations. It allows the writer to avoid the ill-advised heading: "To Whom It May Concern." If you aren't sure, call the company to verify your target's name and title; this is probably the most direct way to obtain the names you want.

☐ *Directing Attention to a Skill:* The ultimate question that job seekers must answer throughout their search is, "What can you do for us?" Its importance during the prospecting phase should not be overlooked. The cover letter allows the job seeker to highlight or draw attention to a particular skill or accomplishment that has meaning to the organization in question. That skill may or may not be included in the resume. Its inclusion in the cover letter, however, communicates some important information: that the writer has researched the company, identified the company's needs, and can fulfill those needs. In short, it says, "Here I am, the employee you've been waiting for!"

☐ *Clear Statement Indicating Reason for Interest:* This objective is the flip side of the above. Whereas before the writer highlighted a specific skill, here he or she is indicating where in the target organization this skill can best be put to use. The applicant is, once again, reinforcing the image of being knowledgeable and industry-wise.

☐ *Control and Follow-through:* This objective allows the job seeker to initiate the exchange of further communication. Much of the job search process lies outside the applicant's control. At least some control, however, is created when the applicant mails (and follows up) a resume and cover letter.

The applicant (assertively and diplomatically) determines *who* is doing *what* and *when*. The *who* in this case is the job seeker taking the initiative; *what* refers to future action; *when* is of the writer's choosing. The objective is to give the reader ample time to receive the cover letter and resume and to digest their contents, so the writer is a known entity when personal contact is established.

Now that the objectives of the cover letter have brought into focus, let's return to the opening example and analyze its content.

With the exception of being personalized and staying within the recommended length of 200 words, this cover letter accomplishes relatively little. The sentence offering an explanation of the writer's current situation and why she wants to seek other employment is neither appropriate nor helpful. (The title of the bestselling book, *Never Complain, Never Explain,* by Victor Lasky, represents a critical element to avoid within the cover letter: complaints and explanations.) The letter's style and tone evoke the average book on resumes and cover letters, which *The Resume Handbook* will show you how to avoid.

On the following page is one way the original letter might have been re-worded:

February 18, 1990

Arthur C. Reese
President
Southwest Tooling Research, Inc.
200 Mountain View Blvd.
Santa Fe, New Mexico 80801

Dear Mr. Reese:

I read with great interest a recent article in Engineering Today entitled "Southwest Tooling's Push to Maintain Engineering Excellence." The article talked of your plans to increase your Engineering Research Lab Team. This emphasis on expansion appears to be a positive sign of Southwest's continuing dedication to quality service. I am extremely intrigued by the team research concept you have developed. The motivating force within a research team offers each member a sense of pride and accomplishment.

The enclosed resume demonstrates my extensive, long-range commitment to tooling research. You will also notice my own experience working with the team research concept. It goes without saying that you are looking for the best possible people to staff your growing organization. I feel I can offer you and Southwest Tooling substantial experience and the high degree of excellence that you need.

I look forward to getting together to discuss your open position. I will call you during the early part of the week beginning March 22, to arrange an interview and to discuss my possible involvement with Southwest Tooling.

Sincerely,

Ann Carmichael
Ann Carmichael

This version puts all four major objectives to use, stressing the writer's strengths and value (tooling research and team experience) to the reader. It answers the two important questions: "Why are you sending us your resume?" and, "What value can you offer us?" The length remains within the recommended maximum of 200 words, and the letter closes with the promise to follow up with a phone call. The overall tone is enthusiastic and informative, without being wordy or overstated. It is, all in all, a well-written cover letter. Another good example follows.

October 28, 1990

Mr. Robert T. McPhail
Vice President of Marketing
Lencor Industries, Inc.
2002 Island Harbor
Fort Myers, Florida 20114

Dear Mr. McPhail:

I recently reviewed with interest an article you wrote in Sales Management magazine, entitled "Motivation Through Marketing Excellence." The marketing philosophy at Lencor corresponds to what I have accomplished on a smaller scale on my current assignment.

As you will note from my enclosed resume, my sales and marketing accomplishments, especially at Eastern General, favorably fit your "Marketplace Management" concept.

Because of my familiarity with your customer base and distribution network, I feel comfortable about my potential contribution to your growing organization. My experience over the last three years of increasing sales in my territory by 31% demonstrates my ability to succeed.

I will be in Fort Myers during the third and fourth weeks of November. May we sit down and discuss "Marketplace Management" and my strong interest in your sales group? I will contact you the first week in November to finalize arrangements.

I look forward to meeting with you.

Sincerely,

Wm. J. Adamson

William J. Adamson

Once again, note how each of the four objectives is met with a forceful and energetic style. The writer has zeroed in on his value and how it relates to the employer's needs. His approach is interesting and flattering without exaggeration. He highlights areas of his resume that are clearly oriented toward the job he's seeking, demonstrates a knowledge of the industry, and takes the initiative by stating when he intends to call.

A cover letter is essential to the job search. Its effectiveness depends on understanding the objectives outlined here. A cover letter may not land the job, but it will certainly influence how favorably your resume is viewed. It may even determine whether your resume is viewed at all.

With this in mind, here are some examples of cover letters geared toward the following specific situations:

- Responding to an advertisement

- Writing to a search firm

- Networking with friends

- Covering your targeted market with a mass mailing

- Reaching consulting firms

- Targeting a specific company

- Contacting a referral

Cover Letter Example #1a: *An ideal format to use when responding to an advertisement.*

DATE

ADDRESSEE NAME
AND ADDRESS

Good Day:

The position of Chief Financial Officer, outlined in your advertisement of August 17, 1989, matches my career interests and is strongly compatible with my skills and experience.

The fact that your company is a manufacturer and distributor in both international and domestic locations is of particular interest, since these responsibilities coincide with my recent activities.

As a Financial Officer for an international corporation, I have considerable experience in directing the full spectrum of accounting and financial management activities. Specifically, I have:

* designed and directed the installation of an international data communication network for reporting sales and marketing office activity;

* initiated and designed data processing systems providing significant improvement in reporting accuracy, management control and organizational productivity during a period of rapid expansion;

* directed the cash management and treasury function (including planning and investment of $47 million), as well as all the forecasting for 4 divisions and 15 markets.

Additional accomplishments are listed in the enclosed resume.

My academic qualifications include an M.B.A. and an undergraduate degree in finance. I have been a C.P.A. in the state of Ohio since 1978.

It would appear that a personal meeting would be worthwhile. You can contact me during the day at (216)123-0000 or by letter at my home address.

Sincerely,

Andrew Applicant

Cover Letter Example #1b: An innovative response to an advertisement.

DATE

ADDRESSEE NAME
AND ADDRESS

Dear Ms. Employer:

This is in reply to your advertisement for an Accounting Representative in the Sunday Star Ledger on January 7, 1990. As the following comparison shows, my experience and background match this position's requirements closely.

YOUR REQUIREMENTS	MY QUALIFICATIONS
Three to five years accounting experience.	Five years in-depth accounting experience. Achieved impressive results by reducing costs and improving inventory control for three years. Administered 5-member staff.
Strong communication skills.	Proven excellence in ongoing oral and written communications with clients and staff. Developed and presented workshops and classes. Prepared operational procedures and accounting manuals.
Knowledge of accounting systems.	Experienced in day-to-day processing of complex accounting systems. This includes generating input and analyzing output. Updated existing system to provide greater operational flexibility.

I would like an opportunity to discuss the position with you personally. I will call you next week to see when we can arrange a meeting.

Sincerely,

Andrea Applicant

Cover Letter Example #1c: Responding aggressively to an advertisement.

DATE

ADDRESSEE NAME
AND ADDRESS

Dear Sir/Madam,

I am responsible for $42 million worth of business in five top consumer and industrial marketing accounts.

Your company is represented as an organization that would appreciate the special and unusual talents I offer. Do my expertise in marketing and sales, entrepreneurial spirit, and professionally assertive nature appear to fit with your objectives?

The enclosed resume will itemize my credentials as noted in my most recent performance review. My manager described me as ". . . an outstanding member of the Marketing Team who is recognized by her peers as one of the best."

Salary is something I would prefer to discuss in confidence.

I am looking forward to hearing from you soon to explore any mutually beneficial opportunities.

Sincerely yours,

Andrea Applicant

Cover Letter Example #2a: A letter to a search firm.

DATE

ADDRESSEE NAME
AND ADDRESS

Dear Mr. Looker,

No doubt some of your clients are facing a problem common to many sectors of American industry: how to stay competitive and profitable in a fluctuating market.

Perhaps one of them is looking for a well-seasoned and broadly-based executive seeking to continue a successful management career in the automotive components and manufacturing business.

My years of hands-on experience embrace a verifiable history of cost reduction, quality improvement, and personnel management with small to medium-sized manufacturers.

Some of my successful solutions included putting in motion a quality program (Statistical Process Control) to increase productivity; establishing controls on raw and in-process inventories to increase cash flow, and reducing absenteeism by implementing a point system for feedback and control. I've also improved manufacturing methods to allow direct and indirect labor costs-to-sales ratios to remain constant even as labor costs increase.

Here are a few examples:

* Instituted a system for in-house brazing. This increased first-year profits by nearly $110,000 and in succeeding years by over $200,000.

* Recommended the formation of a company, making new facility profitable and increasing the parent company's profits by 11%.

* Formed a tooling machine company, making new facility profitable and increasing parent company profits by 7%.

Further details of my career are included in the accompanying resume. Should my background fit one of your current client assignments, I would be pleased to discuss the matter with you.

I will call next week to follow up and see if there is any additional information you would find helpful.

Sincerely,

Andrew Applicant
Andrew Applicant

Cover Letter Example #2b: Another letter to a search firm.

DATE

ADDRESSEE NAME
AND ADDRESS

Dear Ms. Bigtime,

Your company is well known throughout the employment industry. I've also seen your advertisements in various publications. As the enclosed resume indicates, my background includes management of several insurance divisions. Some of my more noteworthy contributions include:

* Reviewing entire division's operation and reducing annual expenses by $300,000.

* Improving processing time in three areas by 20-30% without increasing operating costs.

* Developing and presenting several different training courses, with $100,000 in related savings.

I am also thoroughly knowledgeable in cost control, accounting systems, and administration.

My company's recent reorganization and staff reduction has encouraged me to seek a new position. Rather than accept a transfer that would not take full advantage of my abilities, I've decided that this would be an excellent time to look for a more appropriate and challenging opportunity. The company has agreed to assist me in this process.

I would appreciate the chance to discuss personally any position that appears to be a good match with my qualifications. I'll call you next week to arrange a time for us to meet.

Sincerely,

Andrew Applicant

Cover Letter Example #3: A good letter to use when networking with friends and business associates.

DATE

ADDRESSEE NAME
AND ADDRESS

Dear Charlie,

It must be six months since we last spoke. We had discussed our mutual interest in classic cars and forensics. I hope you're finding 1990 to be an excellent year thus far.

My career status is currently in the process of change. I have decided to leave Flaps & Zippers, where I enjoyed over six years of challenge and increasing responsibility. During the past year, however, I've reached the conclusion that I'd be able to contribute at a higher level—and on a more significant scale—in an environment offering an opportunity to apply my strategic planning skills.

My objective now is to expand my contacts and open the door to more potential opportunities. I was hoping to obtain from you the names of some senior level executives, consultants, and business owners who might be willing to review my resume, offer their perspectives on the market, and point me in the right direction. I'm especially interested in contacting a Chief Financial Officer or Corporate Planning Officer.

It occurs to me, Charlie, that you're likely to know some of these individuals, and your willingness to share their names with me would be greatly appreciated.

The enclosed copies of my resume will update you with my more recent accomplishments. If you find it worthwhile, feel free to forward a copy with your recommendation to a close contact.

If there is anyone you'd like me to meet, please give me a call. I plan to contact you within the next three weeks to update you on my progress. I'm looking forward to speaking with you.

Yours sincerely,

Andrea Applicant
Andrea Applicant

Cover Letter Example #4: Here's a letter to use in mass-mailings—for the bottom tier of your direct employer contacts.

DATE

ADDRESSEE NAME
AND ADDRESS

Dear (

The marketplace is becoming increasingly competitive. New companies with new products, old companies with better products, and still more companies with aggressive sales forces are contributing to the struggle.

Perhaps you have developed concern in recent months that your organization's sales force is not quite up to this level of competition. Or you may have wanted for some time to enhance the competitive abilities of a satisfactory sales group. To achieve either of these objectives requires strong sales management at the executive level. This is my reason for writing to you.

My achievements as Vice President for Scented Chemicals are clearly documented. This $35 million division is generating 23% of overall profits, with a 47% return on investment. Do these numbers represent the kind of results you want for your company?

If you are concerned with sales performance, I invite you to take a close look at my resume. You may discover some qualities you like. Here is a brief overview of my accomplishments:

Directed my company to become the major supplier of polymer resins to nine of the top twelve users.

Supervised the development of amorphous liquids to allow for deeper industry penetration (tripled sales in 3 years).

Created a productive, harmonious sales force, decreasing sales costs while increasing sales results (nearly 45% over 5 years).

These are just a few of my noteworthy accomplishments and a suggestion of the contributions I am prepared to make to your company.

Please feel free to call me at (818)123-4567 if you would like to know more about these potential contributions.

Sincerely,

Andrew Applicant
Andrew Applicant

Cover Letter Example #5: Targeting a consulting firm.

DATE

ADDRESSEE NAME
AND ADDRESS

Dear Mr. Clientrich,

Your organization has ongoing relationships with a large number of businesses. Consequently, you are likely to be approached concerning needs that your clients may have identified within their own environments for senior managers and professionals. Perhaps one of these clients has a current need for a sales executive. If so, you may find it worthwhile to review the information I've enclosed.

As Vice President for sales at Aggresso-Tech, Inc., I built a sales force and a significant sales record. In 1977, when I was appointed Sales Vice President, sales levels were at $3.3 million. By 1988, sales had grown to $28 million, with a 58% return on investment.

Under my leadership, Aggresso-Tech developed ceramic gaskets, which allowed us to dominate the then developing market. In fact, we have become the major supplier to the Big 3 of ceramic gaskets.

Should one of your clients or contacts be in need of a successful, proven sales executive, I would be pleased to get together with you prior to meeting them. Allow me to contact you within the next two weeks to determine if such a possibility exists.

Sincerely,

Andrea Applicant

Cover Letter Example #6: Targeting a specific company.

DATE

ADDRESSEE NAME
AND ADDRESS

Dear Ms. Placewell,

I would like to address the topic of cost-effective conversion of parts to powder metallurgy.

You have seen this market increase appreciably over the past few years. To expand your market share, these products must be made and sold worldwide. Setting up optimum arrangements for international marketing and manufacturing is a critical managerial decision.

I have recently achieved a great deal of success in solving this problem through the use of overseas licensing. An integral aspect has been the sale of specialized manufacturing equipment. The substantial profits derived can be used to establish an equity position in the licensee.

In Korea, our licensee paid us a 7% royalty on sales, in addition to an engineering fee; they also purchased $27.4 million in specialized manufacturing equipment. I obtained an option to purchase 15% of the company for $950,000. In France, $17.1 million of equipment was sold to our licensee, generating a $5 million profit. I was able to initiate similar programs in Italy and West Germany.

As an added benefit, I negotiated with all of our licensees for the exclusive rights to purchase their products for sale in the U.S., thereby benefiting from both their lower labor costs and our advanced manufacturing technology.

As an experienced executive, I am accustomed to P & L responsibility for a company with $80 million in sales, and have managed Research and Development, Sales and Marketing, Manufacturing and Internal Operations departments.

I believe that with my experience, I can help you achieve greater success and explore new opportunities in world markets. Permit me to call you during the week of September 7th to set up an appointment.

Sincerely,

Andrew Applicant

Cover Letter Example #7: Used to contact a referral.

DATE

ADDRESSEE NAME
AND ADDRESS

Dear Mr. Hopewell,

Barbara Contact suggested that I contact you regarding our mutual interest in loss reduction.

I am interested in securing a position in the Quality Assurance department of a dynamic, high-growth corporation where I can expect to be challenged with responsibility. Your organization particularly interests me because of its outstanding performance over the past eight years.

As you will see from the enclosed resume, Mr. Hopewell, I have successfully carried out a wide range of difficult assignments. If you're potentially interested in having someone with my background join your firm, I would welcome the opportunity to meet with you and explore this possibility further.

I will call you within the next two weeks to discuss a mutually convenient meeting.

Yours sincerely,

Andrea Applicant

Andrea Applicant

Chapter Eight:
Personal Sales Letters

The personal sales letter concept is too important to leave out of a comprehensive guide to writing resumes. Not to be confused with cover letters, which serve to introduce and accompany resumes, the personal sales letter (or *broadcast* letter) is a *substitute* for a resume. It is primarily used when writing to selected cold prospects, rather than applying for announced openings through employment agencies, classified ads, and the like.

Because the emphasis of *The Resume Handbook* is on resumes, this section is intended as no more than an introductory guide to writing successful personal sales letters. Nevertheless, the authors have researched and summarized the topic with a great degree of care. We hope you find this brief synopsis helpful.

PHILOSOPHY OF THE PERSONAL SALES LETTER

The purpose of a personal sales letter is to offer an alternative to confronting the reader with "yet another resume." In addition, it allows you to tailor your experience to the precise specifications of the position and the company to which you are applying. This approach is more commonly used by individuals writing to a large number of corporations where they hope to motivate the interest of a key decision-maker, and to explore the possibility of a current or future opening. It is less often employed when answering advertisements or announced openings, especially where formal resumes have been requested.

Like resumes, personal sales letters are intended to obtain an interview. They are, however, better suited to exploring corporate needs that may not yet have been defined. Personal sales letters are thus better suited to seeking executive rather than entry-level positions.

GENERAL GUIDELINES

Always direct your personal sales letter to a specific individual, not to the "Director", "Vice President", or other nameless title. If possible, avoid "Personnel" and "Employee Relations" departments, for they are generally oriented toward existing vacancies only. You can find the names of key decision-makers in the companies to which you plan to write in such directories as: *The National Job Bank; The Directory of Directories; The Million Dollar Directory;* Standard & Poor's *Register of Corporations, Directors, and Executives;* and numerous other professional and industrial resources available at most libraries.

Your own profession may have a published directory — check the library if you are uncertain. A better alternative, though, is to phone and call the company, and ask who is in charge of the department or section in which you're interested. Incidentally, you should also call to verify the names in all but the most up-to-date directories, for such listings quickly become obsolete.

Use standard business-sized stationery, preferably personalized. Type "PRIVATE AND CONFIDENTIAL" on the front of the envelope, or a secretary may open the letter and automatically pass it along to the personnel department, which is likely to negate your purpose.

Do not refer to specific past or current employers, and leave out any mention of current, past, or desired salary. Keep careful notes on all correspondence; be sure you have a quick, efficient way to locate a specific file when someone to whom you've written calls unexpectedly.

CONTENT OF THE PERSONAL SALES LETTER

□ *Opening Paragraph*

Your opening paragraph is the attention-grabber; it must capture the reader's curiosity and entice him or her to continue reading. Unusual, intriguing information related to your objectives is a solid bet:

- I increased the output of my department 212% while reducing manpower hours.

- I made a successful living in South America for seven years by selling African coffee in Brazil.

- As R&D Director of a major manufacturer of electronic testing instruments, I initiated the development of four highly-regarded products.

- How often does one have the opportunity to engage the services of an account executive who recently captured a $1.5 million contract from a giant competitor?

- My professors referred to my final MBA project in financial modeling (just completed) as "brilliant" and "innovative." One of them suggested that an organization of your prominence in the industry could certainly make use of an honors graduate like myself, following my graduation this coming June.

□ *Second Paragraph*

The second paragraph tells the reader why you are writing to him or her. It identifies the specific job you're aiming for, concentrating on a single, carefully-researched objective:

- This letter is intended to introduce me and to explore your potential need for a bilingual petroleum engineer who is quite willing to relocate. If you do happen to be looking for someone with my qualifications . . .

- I am writing because I anticipated that you might have need of someone with my unusual blend of qualifications in biomedical marketing research. Should this be the case . . .

- My purpose in contacting you directly is to inquire whether you anticipate a need for an executive recruiter with a good deal of experience in the academic publishing industry. If so . . .

☐ *Third Paragraph*

This paragraph is calculated to create a desire for what you have to offer. You may state what you've accomplished in the field in question, or list similar functions that support the kind of job you're seeking. Describe outstanding achievements (from your resume) which directly support the job objective. Use short, direct sentences. Avoid imprecise adjectives like "incredible" or "terrific." Cite specific figures. Don't hesitate to say:

- I accomplished/achieved/succeeded in . . .

- I have received six patents, with 11 pending, on . . .

- I saved my company $3.2 million by reducing . . .

- As Director of Marketing of a small company, I increased sales by . . .

- My architectural design was selected and, under my direction, implemented . . .

□ *Fourth Paragraph*

State specific, positive facts about your education and other qualifications that can be verified. Include dates only if potentially useful to you:

- MS (with honors) in Management from the University of Michigan. I majored in Personnel Relations, and minored in Industrial Psychology.

- In 1989, I passed the 10th (final) actuarial exam for New York State.

- I authored the 120-page "Guide to XYZ Information Retrieval" (published by XYZ, Inc., 1988).

□ *Fifth Paragraph*

The final paragraph tells the addressee what action you suggest on his or her part, or what may be expected from you. Let them know when and where you can be conveniently contacted:

- It would be my pleasure to offer you additional details regarding my qualifications during an interview. You can reach me most evenings and weekends at the above number. I am looking forward to hearing from you at your earliest convenience.

- I hope to hear from you prior to June 1, at which date I am expected to make a decision as to whether I will remain . . .

- I plan to be in Chicago the week of February 2-6. In the event that you would like to arrange an interview during this period, you can reach me at my home (212/ 123-4567) after 6:30 most evenings throughout the month of January.

Then sign the letter.

To further familiarize you with personal sales letters, two well-written examples follow. Note that they are both one-page documents, a length we regard as preferable, but not absolutely mandatory. We do, however, consider anything over a page-and-a-half as treading on very dangerous ground.

CAROLE CORRAL
133 Charter Boulevard
Berkley, Michigan 48077

January 1, 1990

Mr. James Masterson
President
Romar Corporation
3303 Euclid
Cleveland, Ohio 44114

Dear Mr. Masterson:

Employed as a Personnel Representative for an international, medium-sized insurance company, I assisted in the development of the corporate personnel department. With the use of a centralized system of recruiting, interviewing, and selection procedures, I reduced turnover 30% over an 18-month period.

I am writing to you because your company may be in need of a personnel professional with my two plus years of experience, education, and training. If so, you may be interested in some of my accomplishments:

* Researched and wrote a comprehensive, 88-page employee handbook, which included corporate policies and employee benefits.

* Wrote corporate salary and wage policy, conducted salary surveys, and prepared and updated job descriptions.

* Administered company benefits program including insurance and retirement programs for exempt and non-exempt personnel. Maintained effective verbal and written communications with insurance underwriters for revision and coordination of medical benefits.

* Responsible for collecting and reporting data on turnover, salary administration, EEO, and pension programs.

* Wrote a comprehensive employee training manual for a non-profit health care facility; this was distributed nationally to other health centers.

I received my BS in Management with a concentration in Human Resources Management from Oakland University. I seek a challenge and an opportunity where I can learn and advance within the personnel field.

It would be a pleasure to review my qualifications with you in a personal interview at your convenience. You can reach me after 5 p.m. at 414/555-0280. I look forward to the opportunity to discuss career opportunities with you.

Sincerely,

Carole Corral

Carole Corral

EDWARD EDWARDS
921 Marshbank Road
Marshall, Idaho 09117

January 2, 1990

Mr. William Tell
General Manager
MacIntosh Engineering
1400 Comstock
Mahwah, New Jersey

Dear Mr. Tell:

In the last 35 months, I have successfully designed, installed, and made operational a computer-controlled, visually-activated robotics system. This system has already saved my firm $275,000, with additional second year savings anticipated to be nearly $560,000.

I am writing to you at this time because of my strong interest in your robotics efforts, especially in visual scanning applications. Your pioneering research complements mine and has prompted me to contact your organization. Permit me to list some additional accomplishments:

* Received the John A. Cartwright Award as Research Engineer of the Year, Stamford, Connecticut Chapter.

* Published article: "Light Shading Activators in Visual Sensing Devices," Journal of Electrical Engineers, December 1986.

* As Director of Research, 1984, improved on-time completion of scheduled projects 39% my first year, thereby saving $135,000 in early bid placements.

* Successfully turned around an historically mismanaged, unprofitable production facility within 18 months; turned a net profit, reduced 50% plus turnover record by half, and cut absenteeism by 61%.

* Redesigned three major assembly lines, reducing downtime by 115%, reducing scrap by 55%, and improving product quality by 35%. An independent audit firm has conservatively estimated bottom line impact of these redesigns at $2.2 million.

I received my MSEE from Boston University, where I graduated with honors from their night program in 1979.

It would be a pleasure to offer you additional details on how I may contribute to your efforts in engineering and robotics research. You may contact me after 7 p.m. at home (208/123-4567). I look forward to your early call.

Sincerely,

Edward Edwards
Edward Edwards

□ □ □

The lessons from these two examples can be applied to personal sales letters in every profession. Personal sales letters allow you to highlight elements of your background in a more personalized format, and to stand slightly apart from the more traditional approaches.

Used alone, or in conjunction a resume and cover letter, this technique may prove surprisingly effective if the simple guidelines we've outlined are followed carefully.

Afterword

The infuriating truism that "everything is relative" can be — and often is — employed to defend the most eccentric, idiosyncratic, and at times, ill-conceived of practices and notions. In writing resumes, of course, what is good and what is bad depends upon what *works,* and what does not. Results are, in the final analysis, what count.

Certainly the element of chance may enter into landing a desirable position, as is true of every aspect of our lives. But a well-organized approach can minimize the random factors, and reduce the arbitrary flow of circumstances of which we may be unaware.

Our guidelines and suggestions are thus intended as a modest contribution in helping you increase your control over the factors governing a single aspect of your career: getting the interviews you want!

With this in mind, we've shown you the ingredients of successful resumes, with plenty of practical examples. Now you recognize the difference between:

- Relevant vs. useless or potentially damaging information

- Active vs. static

- Attractive vs. unattractive

- Attention-getting vs. dull and unappealing

- Cover letters vs. personal sales letters

You now know how to:

- Emphasize strengths and de-emphasize weaknesses

- Focus on career objectives

- Write an interview-winning resume

Some things, perhaps, are relative, but effective resumes are based on the purpose and technique of a carefully conceived resume strategy. We hope that *The Resume Handbook* has given you the kind of strategy you'll need to help you get your foot in the door.

As we said before, the rest is up to you. Good luck!